WHAT YOUR COLLEAGUES ARE SAYING . . .

Nuance is Fullan at his impressive best—enabling leaders to see what was under their nose with sharp action-oriented clarity. Contexts—of people, time, and place—are such key factors in managing change and here he uncovers the subtlety of "nuance," which is the essential bedfellow of "judgment" without which disaster will threaten any leader. Wise system leaders will buy a copy for all their school leaders and keep a copy for themselves.

—**Tim Brighouse,** England

Discover the subtle power of nuance leadership and get dramatic new results. A courageous and timely book that goes to the heart of our complex leadership times. Why do some leaders get extraordinary results while others, ostensibly doing the same things, simply replicate existing patterns? Blending experience and uncommon intellectual acuity, Fullan explains both the key connected dimensions and the exceptional leverage of nuance.

—**Brendan Spillane,** Leadership Consultant in Sports, Business and Education

I continue to be in awe that Michael Fullan is able to describe and explain so clearly the kind of leadership I am intuitively trying to do. Nobody else I have ever read can do this as well as he does. Fullan, more than anyone else, has given me the language for my leadership over the years.

—**Steve Munby,** Former CEO of National College for School Leadership, England

Nuance is a powerful call for a different type of leadership—one that rejects the quick fixes, oppositional thinking, and superficial innovations that make no lasting impact on our most pressing and complex educational problems. In *Nuance*, Fullan provides a richly illustrated account of

(Continued)

how nuanced leadership embraces complexity and integrates competing forces in ways that foster deep understanding, collaborative learning and accountability, and sustainable rather than superficial solutions. It's not a recipe; it's an inspiration and a call to action.

—**Viviane Robinson**, Distinguished Professor Emeritus,
University of Auckland, New Zealand

If you have been waiting to have your thinking on leadership provoked once again, Michael Fullan's latest book will not disappoint you. *Nuance* raises the bar and challenges thinking about leadership while providing those willing to work for it the concrete examples, actions, and steps necessary to do so. As followers of his work have come to expect, in *Nuance*, Fullan "leads from what he has learned" and artfully weaves together complex ideas into a pattern that accomplishes the "simplexity" that makes the seemingly impossible become possible.

—**Laura Schwalm,** California Education Partners

I have to say that reading this manuscript was like looking in the mirror and seeing something of myself that I hadn't noticed before, or valued before, or even been able to put language to. I feel simultaneously comforted by what [Fullan has] written in that I feel validated and understood and even a bit more hopeful about myself, but it has also left me hungry for more.

—**Marie-Claire Bretherton,** Executive Head Teacher,
Kyra Teaching School, England

I get what [Fullan is] saying about nuance. I mean there are 5, 10, 15 different ways to do something; depending on a particular context, it's going to have a different result. I think [Fullan's] on to something really important. [This work] actually helped me get my head around what I have been doing with everyone in the Toronto District School Board.

—**John Malloy,** Director, Toronto District School Board

nuance

nuance

why some
leaders succeed
and others fail

Michael Fullan

A JOINT PUBLICATION

Ontario
Principals'
Council

A SAGE Publishing Company

FOR INFORMATION:

Corwin

A SAGE Company

2455 Teller Road

Thousand Oaks, California 91320

(800)233-9936

www.corwin.com

SAGE Publications Ltd.

1 Oliver's Yard

55 City Road

London EC1Y 1SP

United Kingdom

SAGE Publications India Pvt. Ltd.

B 1/I 1 Mohan Cooperative Industrial Area

Mathura Road, New Delhi 110 044

India

SAGE Publications Asia-Pacific Pte. Ltd.

18 Cross Street #10-10/11/12

China Square Central

Singapore 048423

Printed in the United States of America

ISBN 978-1-5443-0992-7

Publisher: Arnis Burvikovs

Development Editor: Desirée A. Bartlett

Senior Editorial Assistant: Eliza Erickson

Production Editor: Melanie Birdsall

Copy Editor: Lynne Curry

Typesetter: Hurix Digital

Proofreader: Caryne Brown

Indexer: Kathleen Paparchontis

Cover Designer: Scott Van Atta

Marketing Manager: Sharon Pendergast

This book is printed on acid-free paper.

Certified Chain of Custody

SUSTAINABLE FORESTRY INITIATIVE

Promoting Sustainable Forestry

www.sfiprogram.org

SFI-01268

SFI label applies to text stock

18 19 20 21 22 10 9 8 7 6 5 4 3 2 1

contents

introduction

making the world go round

This book has two related purposes: One is to make the case that society in general is worsening and that education in particular is less effective at its main role of producing better citizens. The second purpose is to identify the characteristics of the new kind of leader who will be required—one who can get beneath the surface and help us understand and leverage deep change for the better. I call such leaders *nuanced* because they learn and grasp how things work, and then help themselves and others figure out how to make them work better. They help us see the trees and the forest simultaneously. They know how to mobilize the most people and the best knowledge for solving complex problems. This book will show you what nuanced leaders do and how you can learn from and with them.

I recently completed my "professional autobiography" in a Routledge series edited by Andy Hargreaves and Pak Tee. I titled it *Surreal Change: The Real Life of Transforming Public Education.* I said in that preface that I was immediately stimulated to write two other books in parallel with *Surreal.* One was *Nuance;* the other was *System Change: The Devil Is in the Details,* on which I asked my colleague Mary Jean Gallagher to be lead author because she and I had been working on system change in Ontario, Victoria, Australia and elsewhere. Well, "nuance," and the "devil" never got written during the completion of "surreal," but they lingered in my mind.

Now we have the first of the two (with the devil nipping at its heels). *Nuance* is where I have been heading since at least 2010. Increasingly, I became drawn to applied problem solving on a large scale—what I came to call "whole system change"—something you cannot master without the insights of nuance. One of Pasi Sahlberg's doctoral students, Raisa Ahtiainen (2017), recently completed her doctoral dissertation, titled

Shades of Change in Fullan's and Hargreaves' Models. Ahtianen observed that my pre-2010 writings reflected the "overwhelmingness" and chaotic nature of change and that my approach in 2010 was different:

> Things are still complex, but now they have been approached in a manner that is clearer, perhaps more practice oriented and not so desperate. Thus . . . factors related to managing and confronting change seemed to become simpler, yet the change remains demanding. (p. 129)

Yes, simpler but demanding; subtle but sure. It was in 2010 that I published *Motion Leadership. Motion Leadership* was about how leaders go about "causing change for the better" and was my first attempt at nuance, although I didn't use that term. I offered a few unique insights arising from our applied work, such as "beware of fat plans"; "excitement prior to implementation is fragile"; and "communication during implementation is paramount." Almost a decade later the need for nuance is even greater, because we are tackling *system change*—something that has to be approached indirectly but nonetheless explicitly. The challenge now is how leaders become clearer as complexity increases. Leaders don't become more clear by becoming direct or louder in their messages. Nuance is the answer.

> Any decision that requires judgment, getting people on board, drawing on local knowledge, ingenuity, commitment, etc., requires nuanced leadership that gets beneath the surface to problem solve throughout the process of discernment.

Nuanced leadership is needed in all facets of society because situations are becoming increasingly complex. Yes, there are more opportunities, but there is also more danger that things could go destructively wrong. In the field of education, it is becoming increasingly evident that conventional schooling is no longer up to the challenges that face learners in the 21st century. Indeed, even high school and college graduates in good standing may not fare well in the current economic climate, let alone for the young people who are increasingly alienated from school or who never felt they belonged in the first place. Leaders who can be effective under these increasingly difficult odds will be required in droves. Not all decisions require nuance—some, even big ones, may just require decisive action. But anything that requires judgment, getting people on board, drawing on local knowledge, ingenuity, commitment, i.e., most decisions, requires leadership that gets beneath the surface to problem solve throughout the process of discernment.

Keep in mind that my argument for more nuanced leadership applies to both the macro level of societal development and the micro level of education systems. At the macro level, societies have been deteriorating on key indicators for some 40 years. Income gaps grow incredibly larger, climate worsens, jobs become scarce, technology has a life of its own, and people are superficially more reachable, but empathetically more distant from each other. Wilkinson and Pickett (2019) continue to analyze the trends and find a downward spiral. Their book, *The Inner Level: How More Equal Societies Reduce Stress, Restore Sanity, and Improve Everyone's Well-Being*, spells out the details, except for the fact that they prove the opposite: societies are becoming decidedly and relentlessly less equal. The resulting trend is greater stress for all, worse health, less trust, and the erosion of social cohesion. Eventually greater inequality adversely affects the vast majority of the population, including those at the top (Wilkinson & Pickett, 2019, p. xxi).

Thus, throughout *Nuance* I have in mind how societies are becoming less and less equal, calling for more nuanced leadership that can get below the surface to reshape and redirect the trends. At the micro or subsystem level, I focus on education because deeper, better, more equal, and more widespread education is the most powerful antidote that we have for restoring health to humankind and its condition. Indeed, education leaders have both a micro (how do I improve the local situation?) and macro (how do I reverse the trend of inequity in society?) role to play. I will furnish several concrete and detailed examples of nuanced leadership in action that give us a degree of clarity and direction for changing our future for the better. I have no hesitation in saying that we are at a vital watershed time in our evolution. The period 2019–2030 will be crucial, with the clock ticking ever more loudly as we go.

There is a lot about the process of change in this book—ideas about how to get to desired destinations, including how to change routes when necessary. There is also a lot of content: how to develop global citizens, strong practical skills, deep knowledge, and fulfill humanity, including the crucial equity goal where everyone learns as achievement grows and the gap in performance between groups diminishes.

The good news is that nuanced leaders can teach others to be nuanced. But we have to get inside the process of change and break the cycle of surface change. We have to make nuance more accessible. The purpose of this book is to do just that. Nuance is definable. All I ask is that you be prepared to open your mind and cultivate the *three habits of nuance* that I take up in the upcoming chapters: **joint determination, adaptability, and culture-based accountability**. Remember one vital matter: nuance is about new cultures and ways of thinking and acting; it is not following a checklist or set of steps.

My message is to surprise yourself and others by becoming a more nuanced leader. Master the three habits of nuance but above all internalize their deeper meaning. We will work through a number of specific examples relative to each trait in subsequent chapters. We will have clear conclusions about the need and nature of nuance in the educators' sectors around the world. In the final chapter, I will return to the global picture. Nuance leaders by definition pay careful attention to the big and the small pictures, and to their interconnections. Nothing critical goes unnoticed. In numbers, these leaders make the world go round.

the nature and need for nuance

NUANCE: A SUBTLE DIFFERENCE IN OR SHADE OF MEANING, EXPRESSION, OR SOUND

Have you ever known someone who is technically smart and strategically dumb? Leaders who have good ideas but are politically naïve? Or what about a person who uses a particular change strategy and succeeds marvelously, while another person uses the same model and fails miserably? How about someone who works extremely hard and gets nowhere compared to another person who puts in half the time, but gets twice as far? The difference may be nuance. People who do not appreciate nuance are unwittingly

1

satisfied with superficiality. As society gets more complex, leaders yearn for clarity because their followers demand it. This is the trap that is becoming more and more evident. They become susceptible to off-the-shelf solutions. Leaders who seek or are vulnerable to such solutions (the majority of leaders) inevitably fail. Nuance's answer is don't seek the obvious; seek meaning with your people. Once you find it, it becomes more clear, deeper and lasting. It becomes, in a word, *learning* that sticks.

SURFACERS VS. NUANCERS

In the field of education, almost every school district believes it is doing the right thing: having a vision, endorsing student and teacher standards, considering data on student learning, implementing professional learning communities, and so on. Yet most districts are not accelerating student achievement. Then there are a few school districts that focus on elements similar to those of the unsuccessful districts, but they pursue them differently—more like principles to guide the discovery of specific actions that bring results. In this book we are going to examine the difference between these two types of leadership. I am going to call the first type of leader—a bit unfairly—the *surfacers*. They don't necessarily want to be at this level of superficiality, but they don't know what else to do. Indeed, they may not even know that they are reinforcing a backward trend where things worsen.

> Surfacers treat problems as "technical"—if only we can get the right stepwise solutions. Nuancers work with key "principles" that lead to adjustable actions.

The second type I will refer to as the *nuancers*. Surfacers treat problems as technical—if only we can get the right stepwise solutions. Nuancers work with key principles that lead to adjustable actions. This parallels the fundamental distinction made by Ron Heifetz and Marty Linsky (2017) between technical and adaptive challenges that I will take up more clearly with respect to leading successful change in schools and school systems. Trick question: when you reveal a nuance, does it cease being a nuance? The answer is no. A nuance is not grasped by naming it. You must get inside it and learn its inner meaning in action—and that takes time and skill. We will find that becoming good with nuance is a conceptual and practical skill that requires immersive, reflective action. Each situation is different; one's own situation is constantly changing due to internal and external dynamics. Nuance is called for at every turn. Once you internalize the ideas in this book they become second nature. They can have an amoeba-like quality that adapts to each situation. You still need to reflect and articulate your leadership principles, if for no other reason than you want to self-improve and be a valuable mentor to others. You will need all of this and more as you head toward 2020, and beyond.

I am going to spend a fair amount of time in this first chapter defining what nuance is and is not. By definition nuance is tricky—a kind of "if you have to define it, you don't have it." Ironically, the danger is, once defined, nuance can be applied in a mechanical manner. By contrast, nuance involves the capacity to see patterns below the surface. In this first chapter we will get a strong feel for what it means to be a nuanced leader. I will provide concrete examples throughout the book from leaders whom I interviewed that I considered to be nuanced leaders who were effective in tackling deeply complex problems in their work. I was simultaneously encouraged and worried about their reaction to the interviews. Upon reading parts of the draft manuscripts, those I had interviewed said, "Your questions uncovered leadership qualities in me that I did not know I had." Marie-Claire Bretherton from England, whom we will meet in Chapter 2, said:

> I have to say that reading this was like looking in the mirror and seeing something of myself that I hadn't noticed before, or valued before, or even been able to put language to. I feel simultaneously comforted by what you have written in that I feel validated and understood and even a bit more hopeful about myself, but it has also left me hungry for more. (personal communication, May 19, 2018)

So, what's the worry? Leaders who are already nuanced will find the book additionally revealing, but the danger is that those not so nuanced will not get it, and as such implement the main findings in a superficial manner. All I ask of the reader is to keep this worry in mind as we work through the essence of nuance in the rest of the book.

To get us started I offer the example of Leonardo da Vinci. A key dimension of nuance is to be able to see the big picture—the *system*—while at the same time being able to understand the details and their connections and hidden patterns operating within the system itself. Such leaders comprehend and influence the dynamics of such change in the service of measurable improvements. Let's travel back 600 years.

LEONARDO DA VINCI: THE PATRON SAINT OF NUANCE

Walter Isaacson (2017) has furnished us with a wonderful new biography of Leonardo da Vinci, the renaissance polymath who was "the master of all trades, the jack of none." How did he become accomplished at so many things? Early in his book Isaacson gives the reader the basic insight of how Leonardo became so good at what he did. Leonardo called himself a "discepolo della sperientia" which Isaacson translates as a "disciple of experience and experiment" (p. 17). Leonardo's modus operandi was: "First, I shall do experiments before I proceed further, because my intention is to consult experience first and then with reasoning show why such experience is bound to operate in such a way" (p. 18). He was a person of detail, but more for leverage than for limits: "true creativity involves the ability to combine observation with imagination, thereby blurring the border between reality and fantasy" (p. 261).

On the one hand, Leonardo's advice was to start with details: "if you wish to have a sound knowledge of the forms of objects, begin with the details of them, and do not go on to the second step until you have the first well fixed in memory" (p. 520). He dissected human cadavers—sinews, nerves, bones—so that in his paintings "it is not difficult to understand where each muscle is beneath" (p. 212). He wanted detail so that his ideas could be free to expand: "his observation skills colluded with rather than conflicted with his imaginative skills" (p. 264). Being grounded is a necessary condition for being innovative. Details and *their connections* enabled Leonardo to *see the system* at work.

There is a critical paradox here for our purposes. You need understanding of detail to have overall nuance! It is the key specifics and how they interact that allow us to grasp what makes something tick. Nuance *is* subtle—the exact opposite of superficial. Nuanced detail is efficient because it enables one to comprehend a great deal by knowing the inner workings of the patterns. This may seem a long way from the Mona Lisa's smile, but it is not. Understanding what lay beneath enabled Leonardo to capture what Isaacson calls "the uncatchable smile" (p. 490). Looked at from one angle it doesn't look like a

> You need understanding of detail to have nuance! It is key specifics and how they interact that allow us to grasp what makes something tick.

smile. From another it does: "the result is a smile that flickers brighter the less you search for it" (p. 490). Observes Isaacson, "most miraculously, she seems aware—conscious—both of us and of herself" (p. 493).

We see in Leonardo that nuance is sometimes elusive, but often intriguing—that detail can be liberating when linked to a higher purpose and that purposeful experience is the bedrock of insights. Above all, though, you have to get behind the curtain to see the play. For our purposes the conclusion is that you can never fully understand something from its outer manifestations. But with nuance you have a chance of knowing more. With ever expanding complexity bordering on chaos, leaders will need even greater nuance than the present.

NUANCE: NEVER MORE NEEDED THAN NOW

There is an obvious and deeper reason why nuanced leadership will be essential and urgent. The obvious one that I mentioned earlier as a growing macro crisis is that society is becoming much more complex along with strong signs that life is deteriorating. David Brooks, the *New York Times* Op-Ed columnist, wrote a recent piece where he argued that the current system unwittingly encourages what he calls "five ruinous beliefs":

1. Exaggerated faith in intelligence

2. Misplaced faith in autonomy

3. Misplaced notion of the self

4. Inability to think institutionally

5. Misplaced idolization of diversity (Brooks, 2018)

As Brooks argues, intelligence favors intellect over feelings; excessive autonomy privileges the individual; preoccupation with the self, which values human over social capital; neglecting institutions (governments, schools, corporations) honors the short-term; and idolizing diversity becomes an endpoint not the midpoint to a greater more integrated society.

At present there are more pieces, more unplanned interactive factors at play than ever before. One doesn't have to be a genius to conclude that complexity itself is becoming more complex. Joshua Cooper Ramo's (2016) *Seventh Sense* shows in great detail how networks have become ubiquitous, helter-skelter, impersonal and unpredictable. These "*hidden* lines of network power" can be used to build or destroy (p. 12, italics added). The "seventh sense" consists of the ability to connect with networks to see and feel "forces that are invisible to most of us" (sounds like a job for the nuanced leader). Humankind's possible destruction, argues Ramo, boils down to two groups: those ignorant of networks, and those ignorant of humanity (p. 300). In the subsequent chapters I will show how nuanced leaders come to the rescue as experts in both networks and humanity.

We have more unknowns to worry about: the increasing prevalence of robots is scary and it is not just because of the "uncanny valley" (when robots become so humanlike they leave us with a weird sense of discomfort). Martin Ford's (2015) *The Rise of the Robots* argues that machines are "turning into workers" and that "the line between the capability of labor and capital is blurring like never before" (p. xii). Ford's chilling prediction is that there is no known cure:

> The unfortunate reality is that a great many people will do everything right—at least in terms of pursuing higher education and acquiring skills, and yet will still fail to find a solid foothold in the new economy. (p. xvi)

Consider also McAfee and Brynjolfsson's (2017) *Harnessing the Digital World* where the authors analyze the explosive and interactive development of *machines, platforms, and crowds*. Machines consist of the expansive capabilities of digital creations; platforms involve the organization and distribution of information; and crowds refer to "the startlingly large amount of human knowledge, expertise, and enthusiasm distributed all over the world and now available, and able to be focused, online" (p. 14). The authors then couple the three forces into pairs: "minds and machines," "products and platforms," and "the core existing knowledge, and capabilities and the crowd." They suggest that successful enterprises will be those that integrate and leverage the new triadic set to do things very differently than what we do today. If we don't learn this new way of learning and working, we "will meet the same fate of those that stuck with steam power" (p. 24).

In a word, society is in danger of going to hell in a handbasket. We can no longer depend on evolution to ensure that we come out on top. Actually, the evolutionary odds may be altering in favor of the likelihood of disaster whether through climate change, nuclear button pushing, or the sheer capacity for humans to self-destruct. Humanity has always been able to cope with, indeed take advantage of radical changes, through its own individual and especially group ingenuity. But this time it might be different. Looking back four billion years with increasing focus on the past 10,000 years, the neuroscientist Antonio Damasio shows a trend of increasing closeness of humans to each other. *Until now*. His book title tells us that something different is afoot: *The Strange Order of Things* (2018). Damasio shows how humankind could always rely on the brain to adapt, connect with others and arrive at ever-higher levels of functioning. Homeostasis is his term for this recurring process that

> has guided non-consciously and non-deliberately, without prior design, the selection of biological structures and mechanisms capable of not only maintaining life but also advancing the evolution of species. (p. 26)

It is this process that allows us to claim century after century that life has gotten better on the average for the human race. We do know empirically that life has improved for most people over time over the past 10,000 years. As Damasio puts it:

> Barbarism leads to suffering and disturbed homeostasis, while cultures and civilizations aim at reducing suffering and thus restore homeostasis by resetting and constraining the course of the affected organisms. (pp. 174–175)

Damasio argues that historically it is *feelings* that are distinctly human and that arise via the biology of the brain as we interact with the environment. Having feelings is one thing that artificial intelligence (AI) does not have. It is these dynamic feelings that define humanity: "they are essential for us to experience personal suffering and joy and empathize with suffering and joy of others."

Here is the point. Our dependence on the automaticity of good evolution may be coming to an end. All of this is to our good, *until now!* Paradoxically in the digital age humans are more accessible to each other in theory, but more fragmented, and less likely to connect to others based on *feelings*. People become increasingly aware that they are simultaneously closer, yet more distant from each other. Each person has direct access to the world through their portable device, but "there is little incentive to engage, let alone accommodate, the dissenting views of others" (p. 214). We do get more intense within our small groups, but this serves only to exacerbate the distance from other groups.

Here is Damasio's neuroscientific punchline:

> Homeostasis, as found in our individual organisms, is not *spontaneously* concerned with very large groups, especially heterogeneous groups, let alone the cultures or civilizations as a whole. To expect *spontaneous* homeostatic harmony from large and cacophonous human collectives is to expect the unlikely. (p. 219)

I have spared the reader (and me) the neuroscience detail, but I hope you can agree intuitively and experientially that we can no longer depend on evolution to take care of things. We are bombarded with massive connections to others that ironically are increasingly superficial. The greater the coverage the more extensive the veneer; the result is deceptive closeness based on distal divisiveness and non-existent feelings. This is the stuff of nuclear annihilation, and it will be nobody's—no one individual's—fault.

Compare Damasio's argument to Parag Khanna's (2016) non-nuanced conclusion in *Connextography*: "connectivity enables the empathy that guides our ethical evolution" (p. 383). Well, no. Not when the connectivity is shallow and devoid of meaning. The kind of connectivity most of us experience these days, far from generating greater empathy, inures us to closeness. The naïve belief that things will inevitably turn out okay no longer holds. Connectivity or networks themselves tell us nothing about being efficacious therein. Developing humanity has no privileged position in networks per se. We need leaders who are expert at humanity and expert at networks. Consider Damasio's argument carefully in relation to your own daily experience and you will likely conclude that we can no longer depend on evolution saving the day. Indeed, there is a strong probability that things will worsen, and it could happen abruptly.

These trends operate beneath a complex surface that will require nuanced leadership, which evidently is in short supply. Over 70% of organizational change efforts fail. I would have to say that the main reason is non-nuanced leadership. The latter can be effective at getting the *wrong things done*. In a complex, confusing world people can indeed crave fake news that operates as a drug that establishes its own habit. In threatening times, surfacers provide false temporary clarity that allows perverse hidden forces to fester.

Remember that nuanced leadership is one that contains the ability to read between and see beyond the lines. It involves a subtle difference, but one that makes all the difference. Richard Rumelt (2011) analyzes good and bad strategy. Bad strategy, he argues contains a lot of "fluff"—superficial statements of the obvious combined with a generous sprinkling of buzzwords. "It [fluff] is long on goals and short on policy or action" (pp. 36–37). Bad strategy has lofty goals, "but skips over the annoying fact that no one has a clue about how to get there" (p. 54). Over the past few decades, Rumelt states, "there has been an increased penchant for defining goals that no one really knows how to achieve and pretending that they are feasible." Federal education policies—"No Child Left Behind" or "Race to the Top"—come to mind. Note, the more complex that society becomes, the more vacuous the solution. If you try to make me think harder, I'll think more superficially.

Thus, being ambitious by itself is not a strategy. Heifetz's and Linsky observe that in complex times there becomes "a political marketplace for certainty and answers" (p. xi). Implementers rightly complain and demand more clarity—tell us how to do it they say. Here comes a deal with the devil. Leaders provide more direction and steps, while followers end up on a stairway to nowhere. Then comes mutual blame. Heifetz and Linsky call this the natural outcome of using a technical strategy to solve a complex problem. With a technical strategy, according to Heifetz and Linsky, leaders "apply current know how" and "authorities lead the process." By contrast, complex problems require people "to learn in new ways" with the people who have the problem functioning as "the key actors" (Heifetz & Linsky, 2017, p. 14). We will return to this fundamental change principle in each chapter: the more complex the problem, the more that people with the problem must be part and parcel of the solution.

> The more complex the problem, the more that people with the problem must be part and parcel of the solution.

Learning new ways is, well, learning (and thus leading) differently. If you tackle real problems on a large scale, what we call whole system change, and try to understand your successes and failures carefully, you begin to get a feel for complex change. In this book I have tried to capture what we know about a new way of understanding and acting to contend with, indeed, create the future. Right now, global change forces are powerful and ubiquitous. As such they have equal chances of resulting in glory or gory. If you want to be a player in shaping the future for the better, nuance is worth mastering.

THE NATURE OF NUANCED LEADERSHIP

In education we are at a particular watershed moment. Conventional schooling is boring at best. We have known this for some time, but it has reached a point where almost everyone knows it is not working—ask a 10-year-old. Educational entrepreneur and philanthropist Ted Dintersmith (2018, p. 148) finds that most education systems in the United States are working diligently "Doing (obsolete) things better": tests upon tests, learning experiences that have little meaning for the student, punitive evaluation, excruciating remedial work, and the like. In the meantime, the gap between high and low performers widens, and even those who do well on tests are not prepared for life. The world is becoming more demanding at the very time that regular schooling is standing still—actually going backwards as fewer and fewer students and teachers buy into what they are being required to do. Many studies in the United States, the Gallup poll included, show that only about a third of students are engaged in school by Grade Ten, and many of these students are there for sports, clubs, and their friends. Even the high performing systems like those in South Korea, Shanghai, and Singapore are finding that an increasing percentage of their students, and the adults who teach them, are stressed out and worse. The power of the status quo to keep on doing what it is already doing—indeed to intensify it—is phenomenal.

At the same time the good news is that small but increasing numbers of schools and some systems are developing education programs and experiences that are personally relevant, connected to valuable individual and collective passion, and explicitly develop individuals as they "help humanity." Both Dintersmith and our own "Deep Learning" work (Fullan, Quinn, & McEachen, 2018) describe by name hundreds of examples of this new learning that is occurring in pockets around the world. We will feature some of this work in later chapters. In the meantime, a crisis is brewing, not only in public education, but in society as fundamental global problems mount, whether regarding climate change, refugees, social conflict, mental and physical health, homelessness, extreme alienation, or well-being itself.

I would hypothesize that however well-intentioned political leaders are, those using "obsolete" solutions are what I called earlier "the surfacers." They are going after the obvious—more college-ready graduates, remedial literacy, and performance appraisal—and missing the deeper point: they are failing to mobilize educators who can lead diverse groups seeking to develop a learning agenda to produce self-directed learners prepared for complex life, problem solvers, and team players. By contrast, those up for the job will be "nuancers"—leaders who can get below the surface; leaders who have a knack of prying out the essence of complex change matters; and leaders who can work with individuals and groups in a manner that develops personal meaning and collective identity to learn about and transform the landscape at this particular moment in history.

My main question then is what is there about leaders who seem to experience success time and again? Not leaders who look good at the beginning or are popular for a period of time, but leaders who help develop quality change that *sticks*—that has lasting value beyond the tenure of the leader. In subsequent chapters I will identify and illustrate a small number of key traits of leaders who are successful over and over. Traits or qualities that are not so obvious at first glance but that once uncovered are recognizable. I want the reader to understand these below-the-surface qualities, and perhaps react by thinking: "I kind of knew that, but I now grasp it." Nuance is having a "light bulb" or "aha" moment where something falls into place. When this occurs, it may seem obvious in retrospect, but it feels like—and is—a genuine discovery. That's my goal; you be the judge.

We have talked around nuanced leadership and the critical, growing need for it, but what exactly is it? Certainly, it is leaders who see below the surface, grasp hidden patterns, find new pathways to alter and shape better outcomes, and have a burning desire to make things better for the vast majority of people. Against all odds they believe that they can help the group tackle seemingly insurmountable problems. They have a profound belief in humanity and networks of action that will generate lasting breakthroughs.

So, let me offer a more formal definition that will form the foundation of the case examples that I will provide in the coming chapters:

Nuance leaders have a curiosity about what is possible, openness to other people, sensitivity to context, and a loyalty to a better future. They see below the surface, enabling them to detect patterns and their consequences for the system. They connect people to their own and each other's humanity. They don't lead; they teach. They change people's emotions, not just their minds. They have an instinct for orchestration. They foster sinews of success. They are humble in the face of challenges, determined for the group to be successful, and proud to celebrate success. They end up developing incredibly accountable organizations because the accountability gets built into the culture. Above all, they are courageously and relentlessly committed to changing the system for the betterment of humanity.

Keeping our worries in mind (namely that nuance is not a mechanical enterprise), I have identified three big nuance characteristics of highly effective leaders under complex change scenarios: joint determination, adaptability, and culture-based accountability. I explain them in the next section and then devote a chapter to each one, with concrete examples of what they look like in practice. Nuance is hard work, but it is energizing and immensely satisfying. Our positive future depends on nuance because the solution will be collective and because only nuance is capable of sorting out complex dilemmas under conditions of adversity amid diversity.

THE NUANCED LEADERSHIP FRAMEWORK

So far, the dominant trends in leadership seem to be either being overwhelmed by the challenges to the point of inertia or spelling out from above what should happen. Both approaches fail—the more things change the more they remain the same. My goal is to identify the main themes of nuanced leadership and make them more accessible. In turn, this should lead to nuanced leaders developing other nuanced leaders to the point that such leadership gets embedded in the culture of the system. Let me give one general hint as to what this entails: all good things (or bad for that matter) *happen within processes*. This is why we need the habit of da Vinci's detail that I will return to in each chapter. It is time to start "living within the processes of change."

For complex change matters I try to keep things small in number (three or four), mutually exclusive (ideas don't overlap), and comprehensive (they cover the topic). These are tough criteria for nuance; Figure 1.1 is the result. I call this the JAC model: jointly determined, adaptability, and culture-based.

Figure 1.1   Nuanced Leadership: The JAC Model

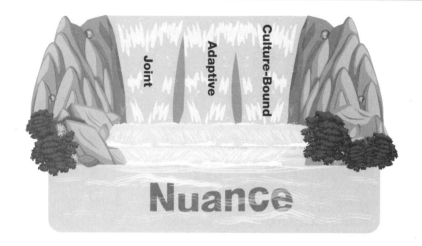

I devote a chapter to each of these powerful factors. We will see that:

- **Jointly determined** change involves developing unity of purpose and action with those in the organization, pursuing and staying the course through continuous interaction.
- Effective focus means that **adaptability** enables the organization to adjust or pivot, to use a modern language equivalent, according to what is being learned.
- **Culture-based accountability** establishes strong mutual commitment and responsibility through trust and interaction.

We have 10 cases across Chapters 2–4 that illustrate these three core concepts of the framework in action. Together the set embeds a self-collective process of effective change. A reminder, though: the three dimensions of nuance operate seamlessly, feeding on, and strengthening each other, thus becoming a *system*. I will return to this fundamental matter in the final chapter. You don't create a signature dish by making alphabet soup! In the final chapter I will also close the loop by concluding that nuanced leadership is essentially a matter of engaging the world to change the world. You have to *be there* to make a difference.

Over the years of being close to grounded change I have identified what I call sticky phrases. These phrases are those that capture an important change phenomenon with insights that stay with you. Figure 1.2 links the dominant sticky phrase with the corresponding chapter.

Figure 1.2   Core Chapters and Sticky Phrases

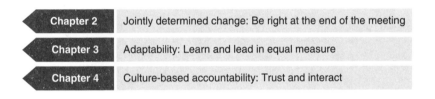

The nuanced leader gets below the surface, sees what makes good change tick, learns from others, and influences the nature and outcome of change by being present and engaged. He or she works with others in determining the direction, gets inside adaptation as necessary, is equally comfortable with individuals and groups as they secure natural accountability that is built into the culture of the organization. Nuanced leaders cause the groups to get better, which, in turn, enables those groups as leaders, to become better.

All of a sudden change has become more interesting. We have our work cut out for us! Never ask an Italian *nonna* for her recipe. Neither will you grasp nor can she explain her secret ingredients or touch. Nuance is an earned quality. The premise of this book is that nuanced leaders get deeper, lasting change because they get below the surface and tap into what activates and drives improvement, while the surfacers spin their wheels as they cavort across the surface. Once they get immersed in given change scenarios, nuancers learn their trade quite rapidly because they are in the center of action having committed to learn and solve problems in real time. As such, nuance is about forging integration of effort. Nuancers learn a lot in a short period of time, while surfacers take forever to go nowhere. Time to find your inner Leonardo!

jointly
determined change

be right at the end of the meeting

Do you want to be a surfacer or a nuancer? If the latter is your goal, the first thing you will need to get over is thinking that you can carry the day by yourself. David Cote, the Chairman and CEO of Honeywell, was asked: "What is the most important lesson you have learned in your years of success?" This is what he said:

> I have a reputation for being decisive. Most people would say that being decisive is what you want in a business leader. But it is

possible for decisiveness to be a bad thing . . . With bigger decisions you can make bigger mistakes. (quoted in Bryant, 2013)

Here is the nuanced lesson:

Your job as a leader is to be right at the end of the meeting, not at
the beginning of the meeting. It's your job to flush out all the facts,
all the opinions . . . because you'll get measured on whether you
made a good decision, not whether it was your idea at the beginning. (Bryant, 2013)

Being right at the end of the meeting is the result of joint
determination—the dynamic duo of leaders and followers working
together, and being open to others' ideas. As we will see, it is not just a
matter of buy-in or ownership, but rather getting the solution detailed and
on the right track. We start in an odd way: what is bad leadership and why
is it so prevalent? Second, how did we miss the wisdom of Mary Parker
Follett, a pioneer in the founding of management studies, born in 1888?
Third, what are some specific examples of successful joint determination?
I supply four examples in particular. The conclusion is that nuanced leaders
have a deep feel for joint determination, resulting in the group becoming
the foundation of success.

THE PREVALENCE OF BAD LEADERSHIP

Sometimes we start a workshop with the following exercise. Get together
in groups of three and have each person answer the question: *Have you
ever had a bad leader, and if so, what were his or her main characteristics
or behaviors?* Then the floodgates open. Try this exercise with yourself;
then with one or more other people. You will find leaders who show too
little or too much emotion, are too detailed or too vague, too smart or too
dumb, too much of a loner or too much of an attention seeker; or who play
favorites, and so on. Barbara Kellerman (2004) devoted a whole book to
what she calls "bad leadership" and concludes that the business literature
acts as if there are only great or would-be great leaders. Kellerman instead

finds that questionable leadership is probably the norm. The bias in management literature assumes that to become a leader is to become a good leader. Already, from the beginning there are two problems: many leaders are well intentioned, but *ineffective*. In reality many leaders have "missing traits, weak skills, strategies badly conceived, and tactics badly employed" (Kellerman, p. 33). Alternatively, there are unethical leaders who fail to distinguish between right and wrong. As we know, sometimes followers go along with the flow, Hitler's followers being the most egregious example. Many an immoral leader has been all too effective. If leaders are immoral, the best we can only hope for is ineffectiveness!

The most dangerous combination of course is "effective and unethical." Some leaders are on the take, and they illicitly exploit as much as they can from the situation, sometimes over decades. Others—those on the incompetent side—may be well intentioned, but are useless with respect to *how* to get anything done. They are vulnerable to off-the-self solutions or what we call the "shiny objects syndrome." If good leadership were that easy, there would be a crystal-clear how-to book.

Alma Harris and Michelle Jones (2018) devote a whole issue of the journal *School Leadership and Management* to what they call "the dark side of leadership and management," documenting practices such as negligence, the mistreatment of people, toxic cultures, and so on. In another domain, the nonprofit public policy foundation *Nesta* presented a report on "good and bad help" (Wilson et al., 2018). We will return to the Nesta findings in the final chapter. In the meantime, in addition to the fact that ineffectiveness seems more prevalent than its opposite, we find that good help is more sophisticated and much closer to nuanced leadership. Bad help imposes solutions and fails to take into account details of context, while good help, as we will see in the 10 cases in this book, stimulates sense of purpose, buttresses confidence to act, and alters the conditions of success. Ineffective leadership is simpler because it stems from the leader, while nuanced leadership is relational.

Finally, one might say that given the growing complexity of societal problems, we need an even higher standard of leadership. The problem is not just bad leadership; adequate or even good leadership is not good enough any longer. My contention is that nuanced leaders are the great ones. By focusing on their actions, we can understand their qualities and make their ideas more accessible (even to themselves as I mentioned in the introduction). The first characteristic that stands out is that nuanced leaders know in their bones that no progress will be made in the absence of learning from and with the group.

JOINT DETERMINATION

We have a long-forgotten source of help from a pioneer student of management, Mary Parker Follett, who came to the fore in the 1920s. Parker Follett was a great student of detail, and therein lies her wisdom. The basis of her insight is that there will always be differences and that the solution resides in the process of *integration* led by enabling leaders. Follett talks about "obeying the law of the situation" where the particular details matter—this is pure Leonardo. The leaders' job in the midst of detailed diversity is to help forge unity of purpose and action (a never-ending continuous process which, for me, is the essence of joint determination). According to Parker Follett:

> The leader is more responsible than anyone else for that integrative unity which is the aim of the organization . . . The great leader is he [sic; it was the 1920s], who is able to integrate the experience of all and use it for a common purpose. (Héon et al., 2017, p. 166)

Getting ever more at nuance Follett continues:

> I have said that the leader must understand the situation, must see it as a whole, must see the interrelation of the parts . . . must see the evolving situation, the developing situation. (p. 167)

Unification is the goal, but it is more of a process than a product.

> There is no such thing as unity; there is only unifying. You cannot get unity and expect it to last a day or five minutes. (p. 168)

> Leadership is fluid because it is always a process: "legitimate authority flows from coordination, not coordination from authority" (p. 171).

How about "you cannot expect unity to last a day." Attending to the process of unifying is a never-ending proposition. Thus day-to-day coordination is the source of legitimate and clear action.

If the leader errs on the side of too much direction, followers are on the receiving end (all the more problematic if receivers go along with it); if the error is on too little direction, potential followers are at sea. This fine dynamic balance is why leadership for joint determination is called nuance. In the rest of this chapter we delve into the dynamics of joint determination by examining four case examples. All are difficult cases, but the fourth one is especially challenging because it involves a case of a persistently failing school under conditions of extreme poverty.

Viviane Robinson (2018) provides the best foundation for a productive form of joint leadership. Being a no-nonsense student of effectiveness, Robinson cuts to the chase by observing that we need to "reduce change to increase improvement." It seems strange to say that no one has asked this question in such a rigorous way. Robinson is also a student of clarity especially when it comes to such complex matters as personal and organizational change. Getting to the heart of our interest in joint determination, Robinson observes that leaders can pursue change through a strategy of "bypass" or "engage." For the former, the leader's "theory of action" dominates. In the bypass mode, depending on a number of factors, followers can either comply or resist the direction in which the leader wants the organization to go. In either case the change is at best superficial.

Robinson was a student of both Chris Argyris and Donald Schon of "double loop" and "reflective practitioner" fame, respectively. Being a sociologist, I studied both of these authors over forty years ago. I never could grasp single vs. double loop learning in a memorable way. Robinson does do this effectively because she is a student of detail. She starts with the concept "theory of action," noting three variables that must be reconciled: beliefs, behavior (actions), and consequences. In single loop learning you contend only with behavior and its consequences (literally single looping back from outcomes to actions to explain what happened). In the double loop process, you loop twice—to behavior, and in turn to underlying beliefs (see Figure 2.1).

> This fine dynamic balance between too much direction and too little direction is why leadership for joint determination is called nuance.

Figure 2.1   Single Loop Theory vs. Double Loop Theory

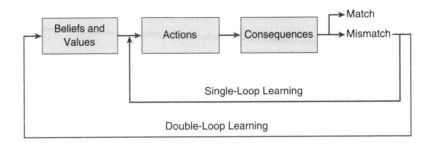

Source: Robinson (2018); adapted from Argyris (1999, Figure 3.1, p. 68).

For complex change, the main problem may be different theories of action (beliefs) between or among administrators and teachers, which the single loop theory never gets to—or at least not in time. Joint determination preempts this fundamental problem because different theories of action and their relation to behavior are part and parcel of deliberations from the beginning onward. This is what Parker Follett was getting at when she advocated the process of "integrated unity," and what David Cote of Honeywell meant when he said leaders must be right at the end of the meeting. They have achieved a degree of integrated unity. This is about as theoretical as we need to get because nuanced leadership turns out to be a matter of practical detail.

I take up four examples here. One comes from the expert herself (Viviane Robinson), and two are from our own work—a large scale example from Ontario involving a whole district of 83 schools, and another from one school I work with in southern California. The fourth example analyzes an extreme case in England: how does one turn around a school that has persistently and deeply failed over time? All of my examples focus on impact so that we can discern the pathways to outcomes.

In double-loop learning, "consequences" are traced back to "actions," but instead of stopping there, actions in turn are examined in relation to "beliefs and values." This process leads to questioning and revising beliefs, causing a revision of theories of action, thereby resulting in altered behaviors and different (better) outcomes.

Case Example One
The Problem of Declining Levels of Principal Well-Being
Bastow Institute
Victoria, Australia

Viviane Robinson recently worked with Bastow Institute—a professional learning institute of the Victoria government in Australia (the following account draws on Robinson, 2018, pp. 87ff). Robinson was already aware that teachers and school leaders find that much professional development is "too theoretical, tell(s) them what they already know, or is not well matched to the context in which they work" (p. 88). The problem to be addressed in this case was the declining levels of principal well-being such as increasing levels of stress and illness.

Robinson critiqued the original plan by introducing the "beliefs, actions (behavior), consequences" framework. She found that the plan was heavily based on input to address new behaviors related to well-being, resilience, social capital, and organizational design. The underlying beliefs were left implicit (and thus were not addressed), both those that might hinder solutions and those that might enable breakthrough results. On the blockage side were unstated beliefs such as "principals should give priority to the agendas of other people: parents, administrators, and other misbehaving students." Robinson states that in most needed change situations "too little attention has been given to the reasons for [existing] patterns" (p. 90). In the Bastow case, facilitators had gone directly to solutions: individual reflection and the development of a personalized well-being plan. What was missing was any reference to the currently held beliefs that principals had about what their roles should be. It turned out that they believed that they should be all things to all people—a stance that made it impossible to carry out their roles in a way that did not adversely affect their stress levels.

(Continued)

(Continued)

Robinson shifted the discussion to examine potentially new relevant beliefs that could alter existing thinking such as:

- My own health and well-being are critical to the well-being of the school.
- I am more likely to be evaluated negatively by my superiors if the teaching and learning are poor. (p. 101)

Related to these beliefs were actions that would have to be taken to realize the new beliefs in practice such as:

- I will spend 30% of my time developing the capability of my leadership team
- I will delegate, postpone, and prioritize administrative tasks.
- I will be more in control of my job, more satisfied, and less stressed.
- The leadership team will be more trusting, more cohesive, and more capable. (p. 101)

This shift to identifying potential breakthrough beliefs made it less likely that the facilitators would waste time on superficial solutions. Instead, the new goal was to identify beliefs that would be related to change in behavior that would in turn produce the desired results: an increase in principals' well-being and efficacy in school improvement. As Robinson puts it:

The primary role of the facilitators would change from that of providing input about resilience and well-being to supporting principals in the discovery, evaluation, and revision of the theory of action that explained their current patterns of time use. (p. 102)

This sequence from consequences to behaviors to examining theories of action, leading to revised theories of action and new behaviors is double loop learning. This approach led to more fundamental solutions, because the "targets" of change participated in discovering the solution. The trainers and the participants ended up focusing on "changing underlying beliefs" (from "I need to serve everyone" to "I need to be healthy to be helpful") linked to new behaviors consistent with the beliefs that were more suited to the desired outcome. The solution was jointly examined and determined using a method that got at root problems. Principals began to question their existing beliefs and actions, recognizing that there were "alternative ways of thinking, acting, and being as a principal" (p. 106). This resulted in new behaviors that significantly reduced stress levels in more lasting ways—behaviors that the principals themselves identified by being involved in examining and questioning their own theories of action.

Case Example Two
Districtwide Transformation to "Deep Learning"
Ottawa Catholic School Board
Ottawa, Ontario

Our second example is much bigger. It involves a substantial innovation and a large organization. The system in question is the Ottawa Catholic School Board (OCSB) in Ontario—a public school district consisting of 83 schools and 40,000 students. The question is how one would go about successfully implementing a radical innovation across the whole system in two or so years.

The innovation is deep learning. It involves schools and districts focusing on what we call the global competencies or 6Cs: character, citizenship, collaboration, communication, creativity, and critical thinking. It requires major change in teaching and learning organized around four pillars of learning: learning partnerships, pedagogical practices, learning environments, and leveraging digital use. Finally, it requires changes in the culture of schools and the

(Continued)

(Continued)

district—basically significant transformation of the whole district—up, down, and sideways. Frameworks, protocols, and other supports are offered to guide the work, but the details and substance are in the hands of the district. We have described this innovation in greater detail in our recent publication, *Deep Learning: Engage the World Change the World* (Fullan, Quinn, & McEachen, 2018). It promises to produce citizens who are part and parcel of understanding and changing their world locally and globally by becoming competent in the 6Cs played out in a dynamic world. So, how would a large organization go about accomplishing such a profound change? Or in our terms, how does "joint determination" work when the joint is big?

OCSB was already a high performing district on Ontario's basic performance measures—literacy and high school graduation—when we began to work with them. Their goal was to maintain this level of success while moving to deeper learning: new learning partnerships, greater engagement in learning, and developing the six global competencies as students and teachers became engaged in applied learning designed to learn about and positively influence their communities.

We will take up the details in a moment. What the results do show is that OCSB maintained their provincewide leading performance in literacy and graduation even though they were immersed in systemwide innovation and transformation of learning. As we will see below, although we don't have comparable baseline measures, staff and students report a very high level of engagement and commitment to working together for deeper learning. The widespread ownership of the new direction in this very large district, I believe, is a function of the joint shaping of the direction and its details across the entire district.

After less than three years of phasing in implementation of deep learning in all of its schools, this is what OCSB looks like:

Academic Achievement Indicators in OCSB

- 90% graduation rate—above the provincial average
- All results from provincial standardized tests are above the provincial average
- All academic pathway pass rates are over 93%
- School climate (engagement with school):
  - 90% of students feel encouraged at school to be involved
  - 88% of students feel encouraged to share their ideas (student voice)
  - 95% of staff feel encouraged at school to be involved
  - 88% of staff feel encouraged to share their ideas (staff voice)

Deep Learning Implementation in OCSB

- 100% of the 83 schools included a focus on at least one global competency (from the six: character, citizenship, collaboration, communication, creativity, and critical thinking) as part of their school improvement plans
- 100% of the systemwide professional learning networks include the use of the Deep Learning Framework in their implementation
- 100% of the 83 schools use the school conditions rubric as part of their supervisory officer school visits, and all 83 schools have demonstrated improvement in one or more areas of the rubric
- 100% of the 83 schools include a monthly update and monitoring component of one of the four elements or Six Global Competencies (Ottawa Catholic School Board, 2018)

OCSB, a diverse big city school district with high performance on traditional success measures, could have coasted but instead took on the challenge of preparing their students for the future. I have already made the case that conventional schools, even if they produce students who are good on the basics, are falling increasingly

(Continued)

(Continued)

short of what is needed for existing in—let alone thriving in—future societies. OCSB took the initiative early—when they did not have to. They involved staff, students, parents, and others in reshaping the nature of learning across the whole district. From the fall of 2015 to the present, OCSB implemented deep learning in seven schools in the first year, eight more in 2016, and all 83 in 2017–2018. They did this in a way where cumulative coherence and commitment developed apace across the whole system. The Director of Education, Denise Andre, and the Deputy, Tom D'Amico, spoke about this journey in a video (*The Learning Exchange*, 2018; https://thelearningexchange .ca/videos/deep-learning-system-level-implementation).

Andre talks about her underlying leadership philosophy:

> We've prided ourselves in being a learning organization, where we value learning at all levels of the organization. I want them to be as creative as we want our students to be. It was an invitation to them to feel they can take risks . . . and to find their entry point where they are comfortable in coming into this particular implementation of deep learning . . . The strategy is all schools, all in. Find your entry point and then from there we will work together, support one another, support everyone in continuing to grow and develop in deep learning.

D'Amico, the Associate Director, echoes this approach:

> We wanted principals to model for their teachers, and teachers for their students. We're co-learners alongside everyone. When you walk into one of our learning sessions, you don't know who the principal is, who the teacher is or who the superintendent is.

D'Amico noted that prior to the current strategy, the district had different departments supporting schools—"all great people working extremely hard"—but "what we didn't have was each department understanding what the other departments were trying to do." We were aligned on paper, said D'Amico, but not coherent in practice.

D'Amico then described the quickness and readiness with which the staff came forth with ideas from all levels of the system:

> There is so much knowledge when you draw on a whole system, and you're not relying on a top-down approach. We may put in some seeds, but the real germination is happening at the classroom level and the willingness to share. They come up with fabulous ideas that we would never have thought of centrally.

D'Amico's observation is key. District leadership provided very few of the actual ideas, but instead enabled school leaders to work with the deep learning concepts and tools, inviting them to develop their own innovations with support from their peers and from the district. The so-called "fabulous ideas" are indeed impressive and plentiful. The majority of these ideas are captured on video vignettes (typically two- to five-minute YouTube versions) and made available to other schools within and external to the system (see OCSB, ocsb.ca/deep-learning). In one example, a special education teacher's class worked jointly with a Grade Four class on the 6Cs using digital resources. The special education teacher observes: "The results were amazing." Students did better academically, and they improved as people, became committed to working together, and developed a greater sense of themselves as individuals.

In another example, a high school science teacher worked with all students to design meaningful tasks, working in teams with room to innovate and present to the group. Students report greater engagement, more self-directed leadership, and increased collaboration and leadership skills. A third innovation consisted of high school students and their teachers redesigning their learning environments, with most of the ideas coming from students. A fourth case involved a partnership between kindergarten and Grade Two students to work

(Continued)

(Continued)

on ideas for changing the world, ending up with a focus on how to support Puerto Rican hurricane victims. And on it goes. All of these examples were enabled by the district, created by the schools, and processed jointly by the system.

How the district evolved seamlessly from seven to 83 schools in less than three years is key. They started with seven schools, one in each of the geographical areas headed by a superintendent. It was made clear at the outset that the deep learning model would spread to the whole system but be adapted to local conditions. Forms of communication, presentations, and cross visitation were enabled. As year two approached, many other schools were seeking to join the initiative, but expansion was held at eight more schools so that the appropriate support could be managed. The system trained "champions" (one at each of the 15 schools, and a team centrally) that supported the deep learning implementation. There were also cross-school visitations and presentations. D'Amico noted that as they approached year three they probably had knowledgeable individuals at 60 of the 83 schools (due to different networks, principals and teachers switching schools, and so on). Every single central staff that led a learning network received training and support from the deep learning champions who led the training and sharing. As part of all this, OCSB reached out to other school districts in Ontario and beyond to receive visitors and share what they learned.

In brief, what OCSB did was to create a new learning system that opened lines of focused interaction vertically and laterally, established that co-learning (as opposed to imposition) would be the norm, and actively supported schools with deep learning changes in pedagogy, partnerships, and new learning outcomes (the 6Cs). The new system amounted to joint determination with focus. Expectations, structures, distributed leadership, and a coalescing vision all reinforced the new direction. When all of these elements intersect, system change can happen rapidly because so many interactive pieces create synergy of effort.

Leadership by joint determination goes slowly initially (seven schools out of 83 in year one) in order to go fast subsequently where with joint determination success spreads quickly sideways and upwards. Top down change does the opposite: it goes fast at the beginning and ends up petering out. OCSB ended up changing the system and the patterns within it. It is worth repeating that virtually all of the specific ideas and innovations were generated at the school level and spread laterally. The corresponding changes at the district level served to support and disseminate the work, and to help monitor impact.

Case Example Three
School Turnaround
Garden Grove Unified School District
Anaheim, California

The third example is interesting because we did it in real time. Our team had worked with Garden Grove Unified School District in Anaheim, California, where the district become very successful in increasing student learning in a high poverty, diverse district. One of these schools was K3 Peters, a very large early learning school. The principal was Michelle Pinchot, whose school success we had filmed. In the summer of 2016 Michelle was transferred to another large school, Heritage Elementary, that was low performing. Michelle and I came to the following agreement: let's see how fast you can turn around Heritage to become a solid performing school. I would only act as a periodic monitor. Every few months from the summer of 2016 to the fall of 2017 (a total of four occasions) I sent Michelle an email asking the following questions:

- What was Heritage like when you arrived?
- What was your plan in the first year?
- How was that plan unfolding at the end of year one?
- What were your strategies in year two?
- What progress is being made in year two? What's next?

(Continued)

(Continued)

I knew if Heritage were to be successful in short order, it would have to be a matter of joint determination between Michelle and the staff. The school did in fact become a fast success, and we published the story in a special issue of *Educational Leadership* on the theme "Leading the Energized School" (Fullan & Pinchot, 2018).

By the second year the school increased literacy and math scores as measured by the new state test in California. The district conducts an annual climate survey that is based on the criteria of an effective learning environment. At Heritage there were dramatic improvements from 2016 to 2018. Figure 2.2 displays the results.

Figure 2.2 Heritage Staff Responses, 2016–2018

	2016	2017	2018
Students feel safe at school	71%	94%	94%
Site leadership fosters professional growth and feedback	30%	86%	100%
This school promotes trust and collegiality among staff	68%	88%	100%
This school has a safe environment for giving peer-to-peer feedback.	44%	93%	100%
Students ask questions when they don't understand	33%	71%	86%

These "changes in culture" are stunning given that they occurred in barely more than two years. How did Pinchot and the staff have such an impact in such a short time period? The answer is that the principal engaged the staff in focused two-way interaction on many interrelated fronts. Here are a half a dozen examples of the leadership strategies that were employed:

Leadership Strategies to . . .

- Establish multiple permanent teams led by teachers.
- Arrange for visiting collaborative teams to observe, collect information, and help solve problems for multiple wins.

- Allow leaders—head teachers or administrative staff—to be highly visible in teacher-led teams and in classrooms through weekly visits.
- Work with custodial and office staff to develop effective operational procedures.
- Use instructional rounds to collect data and celebrate good learning.
- Seed new teacher leadership, including one highly respected teacher who flourished in a new role involving leading the integration of technology and instruction.

Pinchot also benefited from having a focused and supportive district, much like Ottawa Catholic, which helped co-ordinate, invest in, and support the work at the school level. In such systems, district-school development is also a joint effort. We know from other work that principals who participate as learners, with teachers focusing on teacher leadership for improving pedagogy, have the greatest impact (Fullan, 2014). These principals use the group to change the group; they influence student learning indirectly, but nonetheless explicitly. Their nuance is changing the culture of the school as the powerful foundation for changing the foundation of ongoing learning. When leaders like Pinchot self-consciously lead in this way, they get a feel for this method, knowing when to push or hold back; they respond to and cultivate momentum. They build powerful collaborative cultures over four or five years to the point where they themselves become more dispensable because the school has collaborative leaders who can carry on after the original leaders leave. Joint determination has staying power.

All of this is promising. Many of the examples of success using such nuanced leadership involve diversity and difficult situations (more significantly, there are countless other failures where leaders led without nuance and did so using either a top down tough approach or a weak laissez-faire one). But still, can joint leadership be effective in situations of extreme adversity where initial inequity—situations of chronic high poverty and disconnected racial subgroups—dominates? My answer is that we don't really know, as we do not have enough examples of large-scale success under such conditions. Our fourth case, however, proves it can be done through sophisticated and persistent joint leadership working *with* those who need to change (see also the "Shattering Inequity" case in Chapter 3).

Case Example Four
Turning Around Persistently Failing Schools
Benjamin Adlard Primary School
Lincolnshire, England

The three examples I have used so far are ones that at least had some potential for leader-follower rapport. They were still very tough problems that required sophisticated joint solutions from leaders who demonstrated considerable nuance, but what about even more deeply rooted problems that require radical solutions? In a moment we will take up such a case. I was reminded recently how difficult the problem is of addressing situations of persistent, extreme inequity as I listened to the CEO of Baltimore City Public Schools (BCPS), Sonja Santelises (2018). In speaking at the Carnegie Foundation Summit on Improvement in Education, Santelises started with the observation that BCPS had been notoriously stuck in a roller coaster of frustration that appeared to be heading only downward. The system had some 85,000 students and almost 200 schools.

In less than two years, however, Santelises and her team appear to be making progress (although she would not claim that it is yet a success). Santelises et al. developed a "Community Conditions Index" that showed that many schools in poverty had had three or four principals over a three-year period and high rates of teacher turnover. This is not new information. Nor are some of the first steps taken to address it: targeted support to schools in need, getting more qualified teachers and principals in the most challenging schools, forming clusters of 10–12 schools that would be supported to learn with each other, and so on.

Santelises then began to raise new assumptions about change that take us smack into the center of joint determination. She made several new points in this respect, including:

- What if we looked at what equity feels like through the eyes of those living it?
- What if our input is at fault, not what young people bring to the table?

- If we don't look at the data through the eyes of the people it represents, we will be missing something. They might have a different kind of smart. They might have knowledge we don't have if we open our eyes. Think about who is NOT at the table.

Santelises' main point was that it is not enough for leaders on high to *give* people the improvement strategy. You have to work it out with them (she might as well have said through joint determination). This is the nuanced alternative: to get below the surface of conventional approaches to solving problems; to address inequity in a way never before done. The guiding principle is that the greater the inequity, the less effective the handed-down strategy. The question is whether joint determination and related nuanced leadership successfully tackle the toughest problems of them all. Yes, it can; indeed, yes, it must. I consider such an example from England.

Benjamin Adlard Primary School: England

For the last two decades England has pursued a policy of funding what they call "academies." Academies are schools that receive their funding directly from the central government rather than via a local or district authority. Some of these academies are organized into "multi-academy trusts" that are groups of schools, ranging from a handful to 100 or more, working together. These groups of academies are governed by a board of trustees and often appoint a chief executive officer to oversee the enterprise and lead school improvement in some of England's most challenging schools. We are going to zero in on one academy in which a school leader by the name of Marie-Claire Bretherton took on the position of leading a school called Benjamin Adlard Primary School. Her assignment was to turn the school around, removing it from what are called in England "special measures," a status arising from persistent failure with an official classification of "inadequate." The school had some 30 staff, including

(Continued)

(Continued)

support personnel, and 222 pupils. The following account is based primarily on an interview I conducted with Bretherton in June 2018.

Benjamin Adlard Primary School serves a highly deprived area in Lincolnshire about 150 miles north of London. Nearly 70% of the pupils are eligible for free school meals; poverty levels are in the bottom 10% nationally; 30% of the pupils have special needs requiring significant additional support; the school is close to the bottom of the performance tables in the country. The student population is highly transient, with 33% of them coming and going in a given year. In 2014, OFSTED (the Office for Standards in Education), England's school inspectorate, gave Benjamin Adlard a failing grade on every level. In fact, the school had never received a good grade in its history of being inspected.

When the trust asked Bretherton, age 35, if she would take on Benjamin Allard Primary School as executive head teacher, she already was a head teacher in an outstanding school 18 miles from Benjamin Adlard. After some doubt and deliberation, Bretherton decided to take the position. In Chapter 5, I will return to the question of how nuanced leaders develop and refer again to Marie-Claire Bretherton, but for now let's get on with the Benjamin Adlard story.

The typical way that failing schools are "turned around" is to appoint a new leader, who proceeds to replace most if not all of the teachers. Replacing the teachers sometimes works as a temporary solution, but it rarely lasts and before long is a losing proposition, as it depends on an ongoing supply of great teachers from elsewhere— a problem nailed by Linda Darling-Hammond when she wryly observed, "you can't fire your way to Finland" (referring to the high performing Scandinavian country).

Bretherton took over in December 2014. By June 2016 (19 months later) the school received its results from the new OFSTED inspection. Let's start at the beginning. A non-nuanced leader would go into Benjamin Adlard and clean house. Not Bretherton:

I know what I am doing in my own school that works, but I knew that it was never going to be completely translatable to Benjamin Adlard. The context was different, the staff was different, and although the mission and values were the same, the approach needed to be different. I knew a linear strategy wouldn't work. I could have gone in and gotten rid of some of the staff essentially without too much hesitation, partly because of the rapid accountability in England. Or I could have taken the outstanding curriculum model in my own school and imposed it, or transferred some great teachers from my school to teach there. But I knew intuitively that this wouldn't work. I knew that as soon as I brought someone in and said here is an expert who is going to come and solve your problems that I would immediately undermine any sense of them owning the improvement journey for themselves and their ability to learn. (personal communication, June 2018)

To me this is the ultimate challenge in joint determination. How does a leader improve a failing situation without changing staff? The question facing Bretherton was: with a different approach, can you take something that is broken and truly redeem it? The only staff change Bretherton made was to hire an assistant principal named Sam to help her—a person who was particularly good at teaching and learning. Bretherton talks about what she did at the beginning:

I interviewed every single member of staff, from cleaner to deputy head, just asking them everything they could tell me about the school and its history. There were so many challenges, they said. They said to me, whatever you think you know, it is not going to work here, we've tried everything. These children just aren't capable of succeeding in school; the challenges they face in life are just too big. I kept saying there is some good stuff here. We just need to carve it up,

(Continued)

(Continued)

share it, and find a way of codifying and replicating it. At my first staff meeting I said you may think I am going to come in and sack you all. That's not what I am going to do. All I ask is that you turn up every day and that you are willing to learn and that's all I need from you; we'll do it together. That was very counter-cultural and a big gamble. You know we didn't lose anybody. All of them stayed. I think the big challenge was the school had been isolated and the teachers within it had been isolated too. They had no sense of connection with each other, or with schools in the local area.

What you see in this case is the absolute courage of the leader in the face of unknowns. Bretherton did not know if it would work, but she stayed the course and adjusted as the reactions unfolded.

My rhetoric was "we will do this together." I'm not going to come in as a leader and work in isolation with each of you. We're in this as a team so we've got to bring a kind of challenge to one another and support to one another. There was quite a bit of messaging, and there were times, honestly, that I really didn't know if I actually believed it was possible. But I gave myself a pep talk every day. It took me 20 minutes to drive from my house to the school. Every single day I would rehearse to myself about the school. So you know if you rehearse the positive, you rehearse the possible, you rehearse the vision, and it helps you that there is hope. Literally 20 minutes of that at the beginning of the day, because I knew that if I didn't do that and once I arrived at school, it would only take about 10 minutes before I would be overwhelmed with hopelessness.

To anticipate some of the themes about nuance that we see in complex successes, Bretherton used a combination of "nonjudgmentalism" and seeking "precision." Leaders need to be specific, but they can't impose it (partly because they will get it wrong without the group, and partly because imposition doesn't work). Such combinations are the fine detail of nuance.

> Myself and Sam had a policy. For the first 8 weeks we would not give any negative feedback. We literally went on a mission to find anything that we could possibly observe that was good. We knew that as soon as we came in with a hard message pointing out where things were far from good, it would have killed any sense of optimism. We needed to build a sense that there was hope. We had to gently coach, encourage and nourish, and build a relationship with the team so that in time we would be able to give some really specific and clear feedback about what needed to improve, but needed a relational basis on which to do it, and we needed them to know that they had strengths to build on.

Then there was increased attention to what we call in our own change work "greater precision."

> There was a lot of skilling-up of the workforce, first of all in managing pupils, keeping pupils in class, and creating a culture where pupils' emotional and social needs were met. Sam and I felt we needed to do that first because if we pitched curriculum, pedagogy, and assessment first before teachers felt confident enough to manage the room, they were going to get lost. That was difficult because the accountability pressure from OFSTED was very much demanding we sort out teaching first. Once teachers felt that [they] could keep pupils in class we moved onto curriculum and instruction.

Once initial relationships and a degree of trust were established there was a strong move to improve the quality of teacher instruction, and for that Bretherton and Sam used the resources of the Kyra Teaching School Alliance. Kyra is essentially a collaborative

(Continued)

(Continued)

partnership (an Academy) of 57 schools in the local area where leaders and teachers work together to train new teachers and leaders and offer each other school-to-school support and professional development. Once again the norms of giving and receiving help were sensitively considered.

> We had to be very careful in terms of who we brought in, making sure that they came in with servant-hearted humility, competence and expertise, definite skills around coaching and with the aim of building in school capacity. We were careful about who we used and when. We did a lot of personalizing our approach to each teacher. So [we focused on] which teachers were going to be our quick wins, who could learn quickly and raise the bar about what's possible.

In the interview I then asked Bretherton whether there were any examples of reluctant teachers who transformed. She immediately launched into an example:

> I think that some of the teachers who had been in the school the longest were the most difficult to get on board initially, although they are now the strongest and most loyal colleagues. At the beginning there was a significant level of cynicism. One teacher, who had actually some strong areas of practice, was particularly reluctant to work with others within the school or outside the school. He was very competent with the children and how to manage them, but he was also a maverick at times. We used a tool that we created called "teacher tracker" with each teacher to identify and monitor specific teacher competencies in terms of instruction and behavior management [this by the way is an example of what I earlier called precision or specificity]. Sam and I spent a lot of time in classrooms examining the trends. Using the teacher tracker, this particular teacher began to see the

value of breaking things down into quite concrete and specific precise competencies, and that gave him a real insight as to where he was working well and where he wasn't.

The turning point for him was when we said, okay, we'd like you to go and work with the class teacher in year five because you're really strong in competency A, B, and C, and she's got D nailed. Work together. I think he realized that he had something specific to teach someone else, but also something very specific that he could use to refine his own practice further. This also gave them a clear focus. That relationship really began to transform both of them. They were observing each other teach. They were planning stuff together, marking work together, and assessing pupil progress together. They sat eyeball to eyeball and began to really digest their practice.

We also moved other teachers around so that they were working together in similar ways, often in triads. By January-February [approximately a year after the start] teaching was looking solid across the school. We began to deploy some of the teachers to visit and work alongside other schools in the alliance. So we immediately got them thinking about "capacity giving" before they were judged as being good. As soon as you have something to give, go share it. I wanted them to see their role in the alliance straightaway.

My big message is that it takes an alliance to improve a school. In the work of the alliance you see the power of the network, the power of peer review, the power of student voice, and the power of collective responsibility. One of the things we did was to invite pupils from other schools to come in and do a pupil-led peer review, to come into the school and tell us what they thought we were missing. Among other

(Continued)

(Continued)

things students told us: "Your library is full of books for girls. Where are your books for boys? Your playground is boring. It is all concrete. Where is the grass? Where is the green?" So, we brought in students from other schools to work with our students to talk about how they would make our school better, really getting into the detail. That's the problem with OFSTED inspection. It narrows everything down to one grade. I felt like one grade could never capture it.

The OFSTED inspection did come in June 2016, and it did mean to the school something bigger than a single grade. I asked Bretherton what her reaction and that of the staff was to the outcome of the assessment.

Oh, it was the most incredible moment of my life. It really was. We answered the question: it was possible to restore and redeem a school without sweeping it out.

So when I got the chance to tell the staff. I took them to the staff room and everyone was standing around with bated breath. I did a bit of a preamble and then just said, "I didn't need somebody from outside to come and tell me that this is a good school and that you are really good at what you do, but I can now officially tell you that you are good—you are a good school!"

Teachers fell to their knees and wept tears of joy. Some staff described it as a life-changing moment. One teacher in particular said they felt like they could now hold their head up high and talk proudly about who they are and where they work, for the first time in their career.

Putting the school improvement bit to one side, it was actually the transformation of humanity that really meant something to me in the school. It restored professional confidence. It's given them life. It's given them hope. It's given them purpose. The school is now oversubscribed. We've got people wanting to come and work here. We've just announced that the school has won the silver award in the Pearson Teaching Awards in the category "School of the Year—Making a Difference" for its work to Transform the Community.

I then asked Bretherton what she had learned about leadership.

I think I've probably underestimated in the past the power of your own sense of vision and hope, and your own mental discipline, and your own belief. That for me was a massive learning curve. Just being able to conjure up in yourself optimism and hope where you are in the face of somebody who tells you or something tells you that it's not possible. What I learned is about the leadership of humanity. It changes the lives of staff, pupils, and parents. It opened my eyes to the role of a leader in the community. I was absolutely terrified by the challenge. I had no idea I could do this. I had no clue. But I believe I've got enough in me to learn how to do it if I go into it with the right kind of attitude.

I should also stress, as I hope you gleaned, that Bretherton and her team employed a tremendous amount of technical assistance and new skill development. They were careful not to impose it—and therein lies the nuanced skill of deep leaders—but make no mistake that breakthroughs do not occur without major new skill development at the micro level. This is da Vinci's devotion to detail.

> The leadership of humanity changes the lives of staff, pupils, and parents.
> —Marie-Claire Bretherton

Bretherton and I then went on to talk about other matters. How could the region's larger Kyra Teaching School Alliance of over 50 schools, the Federation of Teaching Schools Alliances, and

(Continued)

(Continued)

multi-academy trusts—totaling over 300 schools—be a force for change in Lincolnshire as a whole? We call this strategy "leadership from the middle," where schools help each other and begin to influence policy upwards in the state. But that is for another book on system change, one we call *the devil* (Gallagher & Fullan, forthcoming; see also Hargreaves & Shirley, 2018).

INTEGRATIVE LEADERSHIP

The message of this chapter on joint determination takes us back to Mary Parker Follett. There can be no progress without unity of purpose and action that itself involves a process of continually unifying the sense of collective purpose and the individual and group capacity to make improvements. In complex societies with complex problems, we need nuanced leaders who set out to identify various strands of the problem and are flexible and creative in weaving these elements together in ways that address the various constraints of the situation while making substantial progress. Such leadership is impossible for those who stay on the surface, do not inquire deeply, and want a quick fix.

It is also clear from our case examples that nuanced leaders are obsessed with making an impact. Nothing is acceptable that falls short of measurable success for the people in the situation. I think that the most profound message about joint determination is that the vast majority of people—teachers in schools for example—want to make a difference. *They care!* Nuance leaders unlock, mobilize, and create collective care. Nuance leaders prove that the seemingly impossible can be done. But wait! We are only one-third of the way there. Implied, but not made explicit, are the continuous adjustments that are made during the process. Every situation is unique, which means adjustments will be required, but that is normal in complex problem solving. Adaptability suited to the dynamics of the situation is our second nuanced quality.

> Nuanced leaders are obsessed with making an impact. . . . They unlock, mobilize, and create collective care.

adaptability
learn and lead in equal measure

Let me say it first. Joint determination does entail adaptations so there is some overlap, but it is still helpful to make the distinction in order to highlight the need to refine or change course, or even to reinforce the need for the mindset to make continual adjustments. The ability of leaders to change their minds when a strategy isn't working is not as prevalent as we might wish. I spoke recently to a consultant I know who was trying to persuade a superintendent of a large urban district in the United States to take a different tack to the problem of turning around persistently failing schools in his system. Instead of handing down solutions, she wanted him to engage the principals in co-developing a strategy. The superintendent's position was that these schools have failed the kids (which in a sense they have), so they need to be told what to do differently by the central office. The district team continued to work on getting a complete list of the "what" that should be done and had spent little time to date on the "how." As principals in the "failing schools" waited to hear what would be done "to" them, the tensions began to rise. At least half of the central team saw the problem, but the other half had a firmer grip on the steering wheel. This system was badly in need of adaptive capacity. It had the right focus but the wrong method of addressing it. It could only go backwards—the more things change, the more they remain the same. There may be hope, however. This same consultant recently updated me and said the senior team is now debating whether the selected matrix of programs and associated professional development is the answer—as one of them argued, "We can't PD our way out of this." There seems to be a growing realization that continuous learning will be necessary—a good start but not yet nuance.

Adaptability is a deeper facet of joint determination because it works on combining forces to come up with new solutions not yet tried. In this chapter I provide four examples of adaptive focus that involved substantial changes across whole systems—all represented focus combined with adaptation. The four cases consist of the following: one-to-one computers for every child in a district; how to accomplish unity of purpose and action within the Toronto District School Board with its 583 schools; how to achieve equity in learning within a school that experienced a 25% influx of high poverty, racially different students from the existing student body; and fostering deep learning in over 1,000 schools in seven countries. As we will see, nuanced leaders never become settled experts because they are always learning.

Case Example Five
Rescuing Education From Technology
Mooresville, North Carolina

In 2011 I wrote a paper that identified four wrong policy drivers for whole system reform—wrong in the sense that they did not work to get the hoped-for results. One of these wrong drivers was technology (the other three were punitive accountability, individualism, and ad hoc policies). In effect, I argued that "pedagogy" needed to be the driver and that technology could be the accelerator. The common practice at the time was to the contrary; leaders were trying to buy their way into the future by loading up on technology. It seemed to me that once you start with technology (big purchases, for example) you end up going down its pathway.

Once such person who started down the pathway of technology in a major way is Mark Edwards. Mark served as superintendent of Henrico County Public Schools, Virginia, from 1994 to 2004. He was known as a hero of one of the first one-to-one (one computer for every child) computing initiatives in the United States, in which 26,000 laptops were deployed to students in Grades 6–12. He won many awards for this high-profile feat. As far as I know, Henrico did not show significant increases in student achievement in that period. Mark then moved to Mooresville Graded School District (MGSD— 5,600 students and seven schools), where he was superintendent from 2007 to 2016. It was in the first few years of this period that he had his *adaptive conversion.* Because nuance is subtle and involves understanding underlying patterns that were previously not appreciated, it is not something that occurs suddenly, although its realization eventually can come as an "aha" moment.

Mark wrote two books focusing on Mooresville (Edwards, 2014, 2016). The shift in perspective that Mark underwent in his work in Mooresville is significant. He had started with a commitment to one-to-one computers. In the first instance this often means bridging the digital divide so that all students have equal access to technology. He was also driven by the moral imperative of serving all children regardless of socioeconomic background. I take no credit for the next step in his thinking: He explained that Mooresville administrators read and discussed Michael Fullan's books *All Systems Go* and *The Six Secrets of Change,* noting that "the ideas in these books brought clarity to our purpose as school leaders,

(Continued)

(Continued)

galvanized our team beliefs, and helped us embrace the moral imperative as we strive to live up to our motto, '*Every child every day*'" (2014, p. 19). In the 2007–2012 period, Mark and MGSD as a whole made the shift from digital domination to moral purpose embedded in collaborative cultures.

Interestingly, focusing on high expectations and the moral imperative for all is never sufficient. Non-nuanced leaders identify the moral imperative but do not realize that there is a set of underlying factors that must be fostered for success. In the 2014 book Mark identified several of these factors: the moral imperative, a culture of caring, instructional focus, and daily use of data. But then he began to identify that it is the combination of certain other forces that make the lasting difference. The 2014 book was entitled *Every Child, Every Day*. By 2016, the title was *Thank You for Your Leadership* with the following chapter headings: "Distributed Leadership," "Leaders with Shared Vision," "Aligning Leaders With the Mission, Cultural Conditions for Shared Leadership," "Everyday Pathways to Leadership," "Formal Programs of Leadership Growth," "Leading With Formative Power, and Second-Order Leaders." Revealingly, putting the student on the only pedestal (or in business singling out only the customer as always right) can end up being surface stuff. All districts have "children are first" vision statements. Success becomes evident only when you build the underlying patterns where *people are first* (students and adults alike) as the system helps make them the best they can be. Nuance involves building the capacity of the adults around the students, especially those children not doing well. Effectiveness is multifaceted, and nuance is the art of developing and connecting the sinews of success.

> Nuance involves building the capacity of the adults around the students, especially those children not doing well.

Each year MGSD got stronger with ever more consistent results. What Mark did as leader over time was to shift the strategy from digital conversion, to moral imperative (still at the surface in the early days), to creating a culture of change with multiple moving parts that reinforced each other in ways that were not so obvious to the naked eye. He and the district adapted and consolidated as they went. We see how much attention to detail and the interrelationship of its parts are required to obtain the synergy of continuous growth that was associated with MGSD's impressive success. The good news is that you can identify and see what is needed—which in fact Mark and I did in a subsequent book, *The Power of Unstoppable Momentum* (Fullan & Edwards, 2017).

In April 2018 I asked Mark to reflect on what he saw as the difference between the Henrico and the Mooresville strategies. Here is his response:

Back in 2000 in Henrico County Schools we deployed 26,000 laptops for all middle school and high school students. We focused our work on appropriate use, digital integration, device management and change leadership, but the focus was primarily on "the technology innovation." Yes, we focused on staff development and student achievement, but the "clarion call" to our teachers, students and staff was focused on machines.

Fast forward to the Mooresville School District, Mooresville, NC 2009, and we were providing every 3–12 student their own laptop, but the focus of the work had evolved to a very different place. Rather than a device-centered initiative, we were intent on structuring our work and professional development with a focus on collaborative cultures.

(Continued)

(Continued)

> Our vision of instruction was primarily about personal-
> ized work and team project work. We evolved as a team
> and culture to realize that we had a huge source for syn-
> ergy and energy by cultivating and embracing collabora-
> tive instructional design. We saw a surge in productivity,
> a decline in all disciplinary issues, and a huge force field
> of personal and collaborative creativity with a foundation
> of instructional inquiry by teachers and students. By 2014
> the norm of classroom experience was all about building
> collaborative synergy for students and teachers. The results
> were framed around academic achievement for all students
> but more importantly, [they were generated by] the learn-
> ing energy and instructional joy of collaboration. (personal
> communication, April 2018)

When I asked Mark what specifically had changed his mind, this
is what he said:

> A couple of years into our Digital Conversion in
> Mooresville, we had a two-year waiting list for our
> Structured Visits from school districts around the US and
> world. Most districts came to see a laptop implementation
> that showed promising results. It was around that time that
> a significant shift occurred from the questions and inter-
> est of our guests. Everyone commented and inquired about
> the work culture of students and teachers. We had evolved
> our instructional model to include a significant amount
> of project-based work with teams. There was a visceral
> change in the classroom learning dynamic with a delib-
> erate focus on collaborative teams. The "hum" of student
> dialogue and the independent and productive work of stu-
> dent collaborative teams was what everyone noticed and

wanted to learn about. Yes, the digital resource was central to the work, but the learning was turbocharged by engagement, dialogue, and teamwork. It was an organic revelation for the MGSD team and me that the real engine for purposeful change was collaborative synergy. (personal communication, April 2018)

Mark and his team experienced a fundamental shift in "adaptive focus," or, as he called it, "an organic revelation." The goal of student achievement for all remained the same, but the basis for getting there radically changed. The nuance was not just the nature of the change—focus on culture—but rather on *the constellation of details* that would be required to make it work:

- focused collaborative cultures,
- instructional practices that leveraged digital,
- targeted and ongoing use of data,
- corrective action that motivates,
- celebration of success, and
- continual cultivation of professional capital.

Moreover, all of this had to be disseminated throughout the district to the point where virtually everyone could "talk the walk," i.e., could explain in specific language the strategy being used and the causal pathways to improved results.

Alas, by definition you can never imitate nuance. But you can learn from and appreciate what it looks like in practice. Effective leaders do not learn literally from others, but they can adapt and derive lessons from successful examples provided they can dig to the level of detail. I hope that by getting underneath many examples in this book the cumulative effect will be instructive. Become a student of other people's nuance, but develop and refine your own. The next example is a whopper.

Case Example Six
The Toronto District School Board
Ontario, Canada

In 2013, Alan Boyle and I conducted case studies of three big-city school reforms being implemented in New York City, London, and Toronto (Fullan & Boyle, 2014). We titled the Toronto case "Success Among the Rocks." With almost 600 schools and 245,000 students, the Toronto District School Board was founded in 1997 by amal-gamating five previous districts into one. From 2004, a new provincial government established three big education priorities: literacy, numeracy, and high school graduation. During the next 12 years, TDSB made steady progress on these goals (the success part) while experiencing a good deal of political wrangling among its 22 school trustees and between parts of the school board and the three directors (superintendents) of education who served during this time (the rocks part). The politics became so intense that the minister of education established an independent external review conducted by prominent educator Margaret Wilson. Wilson reported to the minister in January 2015, documenting what she called a "culture of fear" at the senior level of the board (trustees and the director). Nine of the ten rec-ommendations focused on the seemingly endemic misbehavior of trustees. (Incidentally, we just finished a book on positioning local governance [school boards] as a force for positive change [Campbell & Fullan, forthcoming].) There was talk that the board was ungov-ernable because of size and intractable climate and should be reduced in size to four or so boards.

By this time (January 2015) a new board had been elected in November 2014 and took office in January. It consisted of a combi-nation of newly elected members and some existing trustees who had been re-elected. This new board wanted to set a new direction and began to do so in 2015.

Later that same year, November 2015, the director of educa-tion, Donna Quan, made a decision to accept a secondment to the Ministry of Education 18 months prior to the end of her contract.

The board then set out to appoint Ms. Quan's successor. One of the people who soon came to be the focus of discussion was John Malloy. I know Malloy well, as he had been one of the subjects of my book *Motion Leadership in Action* when he was director of the Hamilton-Wentworth District School Board just west of Toronto (see Fullan, 2013b). When Malloy finished as director in late 2014, he was promptly recruited to become one of the assistant deputy ministers in the Ontario Ministry of Education. Less than a year into his ministry role (November 2015) came the exploration from the Toronto School Board's search committee about the director's position.

I'll keep the politics simple here. Malloy and I talked about the director's role, and the idea began to emerge that he would be more needed at TDSB *if* the conditions were right (given the history of ungovernability). I don't know the details of the behind-the-scenes discussions, but essentially the new board and Malloy mutually committed to respect each other's roles in order to support effective governance and to build positive relationships. On that basis Malloy was appointed as director for 18 months effective January 1, 2016; and one year later he was asked to stay for five more years, which is how things stand as I write in the summer of 2018.

Malloy's Startup

As I came to write this chapter on adaptability, I knew if Malloy were to be successful in this behemoth board he would have to be at his nuanced best. So, I conducted a major interview with him on March 30 that focused on his role from January 2016 to March 2018. The rest of this section is based on this interview and TDSB documents (all direct quotes are noted as JM [John Malloy], or MF [Michael Fullan]).

> I inherited a culture that when you talk about system direction, people then started expecting the templates, the recipes, the road maps. (JM)

(Continued)

(Continued)

Note the complete absence of any notion of "joint determination." By contrast Malloy said:

> We need a compelling strategic direction that resonates with people. However, this direction, though it provides some coherence, should not attempt to direct all actions, all behaviors, and all decisions from the central level. (JM)

This is tantamount to Leonardo's modus operandi that I described in Chapter 1. Recall that Leonardo was a "disciple of experience and experiment"; by combining observation with imagination the leader creates a new reality that becomes more and more grounded through cumulative shared interaction and articulation. Let's take a closer look.

> You have a history of people waiting for direction from the top, and a huge number of people all over the place. So, how do you finesse the connection amidst such diversity? (MF)

> *[Malloy's response]* This is what we learned. We need to strengthen the relationship between the school principals and the superintendents by focusing on that pivotal relationship in a couple of ways. First, I rearranged staffing so that I could have more superintendents working with fewer schools each. When I first came to TDSB, we had 20 superintendents working with approximately 30 schools each. I changed that so now we have 28 superintendents working with closer to 20 schools each. Second, we focused our support on those 28 superintendents to work with the principals and schools differently. (JM)

Malloy continued to explain the shift in behavior:

> Before, the superintendents were there for crises; they were there for complaints; they were there for ceremonies and

celebrations and to be sure that our schools were compli-
ant with system expectations. I wanted them to shift their
roles and be supportive in all ways. We needed the insight
and intelligence and the perspective from communities,
classrooms, and schools to influence our system direction.
The system direction itself needed to be made stronger, communicated back and forth between superintendents and the
principals. (JM)

Malloy also reorganized the academic executive superintendents
(there are eight of them) so that they worked in this new fashion
with their principals (in the new system four executive superintendents each had seven area superintendents who in turn had about
20 schools each). The other four executive superintendents worked
at the system level in responsive ways vis-à-vis schools. In other
words, the change in culture being introduced amounted to the system supporting schools, not the other way around.

Changing culture, especially in a large system like TDSB, is
nuanced work because it is a process of subtly, persistently, and
ubiquitously discussing and, in effect, coalescing new details. The
nature, frequency, and consistency of dialogue serves to develop and
strengthen new focuses.

[Malloy continues] So, in order for this to work, we needed
to be sure that the area superintendent took on a different
stance, one where they were truly in schools—right now I
am thrilled because I visit schools with my superintendents.
I don't go alone, and thus I can see the impact of superintendents through these visits. I want superintendents to be part
of the school community that they are supporting in a way
that allows us to move in a common direction. I personally
meet with all (28 + 8) superintendents twice a month because
I want to hear what's happening from the field. Then the
executive team can take this upward information, formulate

(Continued)

(Continued)

how the direction needs to be in hand, bring it back to the area superintendent who again can play this very important role at the school level. These insights continuously influence our system direction, and then we can adjust our system direction as we go in order to meet the needs of schools.

So, my summary is that in order for us to get a compelling direction that doesn't suffocate people, we needed to figure out where the most significant relationship is and how to support it; thus we have been working with that principal/superintendent relationship. (JM)

What we have then is a leader who has taken two steps intended to produce greater focus and engagement. One was a structural change to enable area superintendents to work with fewer schools. The other involves a change in the role itself to enable new two-way discussions about the strategic directions. The third change, according to Malloy, concerns the process for managing the content of the direction. Let's turn to that.

Process and Content

Recall the rather general observation I made in Chapter 1 that "all good things (or bad for that matter) *happen within processes.*" John Malloy knows this, and we can use it to examine the widely misunderstood role of strategic plans based on vision. My critique of most strategic plans is that they lack nuance. TDSB had an operating plan prior to Malloy's arrival. When he began his tenure in January 2016, he noted that there were a great many things happening in the district, but he struggled to get a sense of what was driving all 583 schools. In order to guide system conversation, Malloy and his team created a document called *A Vision for Learning at TDSB* (TDSB, 2016). The subtitle is "Our guide to school improvement and school effectiveness" and features three big ideas: "Improvement for all students; Enhanced learning culture," and "Shared leadership." It is 16 pages long. So far, so normal!

For Malloy, a document is not just a document.

> The third thing that we've learned is that this strategic direction has to be a lot more *about process* that provides some parameters or expectations without necessarily defining product or outcome. When I arrived, the strategic plan had generated some achievement and outcomes by doing many, many things centrally, and I respect that foundation. But it wasn't breeding ownership; some school principals were still expecting when the next lesson plan would be coming from central office. Where we found ourselves when I arrived— and it was the team that told me this—we were static. We needed to figure out the way for schools to own their own improvement. (JM, my italics)

In the absence of movement—in fact, there was a growing backlash in the district to the word *initiative*—Malloy identified the core issue of how to get local ownership in the context of system goals. This he saw as a process problem:

> If we are building ownership for improvement in schools, then we might actually allow the school-based voice to influence us in a way that kind of keeps the system in check as well. (JM)

This is beginning to smack of joint determination, but Malloy goes further.

> Specifically, when I say a focus on process, we expect every school to determine an authentic focus in areas of achievement, well-being, and equity. Our definition of achievement includes literacy and numeracy, but also includes global

(Continued)

(Continued)

competencies [the 6Cs: character, citizenship, collaboration, communication, creativity, and critical thinking]. Our definition of well-being focuses on how we are supporting our students' mental and physical health and sense of belonging. Our definition of equity concentrates on what needs to change on the part of educators so that achievement and well-being improve. We are challenging educator bias and removing school and classroom barriers.

The second process expectation is to determine what evidence are you gathering to show that improvement is happening. The standardized test scores give us some information that's important. I appreciate this data, but it is sometimes given too late for schools to make a difference with the students in front of them. We ask schools to consider what evidence they are gathering to show that they are improving in these focus areas, and then how the school is supporting staff reflection that will inform what is going to happen next. We have been clear about these process expectations; we have supported principals in taking the lead on creating those conditions; we have supported superintendents to monitor impact without feeling they have to take the principal's job. (JM)

In this way Malloy re-created the strategic plan.

I spent the first three months [Jan., Feb., March] listening to people. That's when I learned that we had pockets of great things; we had all kinds of dedicated people, but we were siloed, and that's how I worked to re-create the "Vision for Learning" for everyone. (JM)

After six months—January to June 2016—feedback from the schools and the superintendents was good. The next piece involved the establishment of new Learning Centres (TDSB, January 2017). There are four of them, consisting of a total of some 80 instructional coaches and other professional support services. There were two related reasons for this move. First, TDSB was seen as a big bureaucracy that was policy driven and not very responsive partly because people didn't know each other. The other main reason for the new centers was that the 28 superintendents were working in isolation. The Learning Centres are bringing together the four regional groups of seven superintendents each to help focus on areas of instructional support.

The final structural/process piece is the *Integrated Equity Framework* (TDSB, 2016–2019); in May 2018 the board passed the *Multi-Year Strategic Plan* that was informed by the equity framework. The Toronto District both before and after amalgamation has always been committed to equity; however, the challenge is to ensure that equity policies impact practices in classrooms and school. Still, TDSB has done well for a big-city operation with great diversity—well over half the student population does not come from an English-speaking home, and many Board documents are translated into over 100 languages. Their performance as a district is at the 80% average level on most measures—literacy and high school graduation, for example— which itself is impressive. But 20% underserved, as TDSB calls them, is still high, especially since some subgroups are well below that figure (blacks, indigenous students, special education).

It's a tough problem. Equity policy per se often is not powerful on the ground that it is based on the assumption that the system should fix everything. As Malloy observes, "Compliance doesn't get you very far when there are 583 places that are supposed to implement it." With the data and evidence TDSB has collected for years, it is possible to pinpoint low performance. But it needed a mechanism to zero in on implementation. The district acknowledged that low performance for some groups was a systemic issue. As Malloy put it:

In order not to be pulled in too many directions by all the really significant issues that were being communicated to us, the *Integrated Equity Framework* said to our community,

(Continued)

(Continued)

> okay we get that we have to change something; let us be more focused on those changes. (JM)

We now have some big pieces: the *Vision for Learning*, the *Learning Centres*, and the *Integrated Equity Framework*, and now the *Multi-Year Strategic Plan*. Each has had its own good process. Malloy now sees the next priority as twofold. First, continue to help principals and schools get better and better at processes:

> We keep talking about a school improvement focus, but realized that we didn't teach the process and not everyone knew how to do it. So we taught the process of how do you look at data, how do you know your students, how do you support your staff, how do you land on a really authentic focus or focus areas, and how do you determine which evidence will be gathered to show whether or not you are getting improvement? (JM)

The second key part of process involves continuous consultation with communities:

> We have engaged our communities in order to figure out what they believe our focus needs to be. We are working to keep the emphasis on improvement on the classroom and school level supported by the system even though sometimes communities direct their attention to what they expect the system to do. (JM)

I asked Malloy what he has learned about system leadership given the last 27 months of immersion in a complex behemoth like TDSB. This is what he said:

> People have confidence in the system leaders when we listen, we observe, and we engage. And the most important part

is that we not only synthesized what we've heard, but we are willing to share it back with our stakeholders and *not to be afraid to change if we didn't get it right.* (JM, italics added)

That, dear reader, is adaptability!

I asked Malloy what else he had learned at the personal level. He made several points:

Honesty and candor are so required because people expect big bureaucracies to speak in ways that are not clear, that don't name the issues, that aren't willing to admit mistakes ... You also have to figure out what your guiding principles are based on data and evidence. Then I have to remain hospitable and firm because political factors, special interest groups, [or] emotional scenarios will pull me off those guiding principles on a regular basis.

I also learned the art of patience because early in my tenure there were times when I became a bit overwhelmed by how many pressures were coming my way and I found those pressures stressed me out and then I stressed the team ... my own reaction was causing stress in ways that were not helpful. (JM)

I then asked Malloy what micro strategies he used to handle stress. His first response was "never send an email when there's something intense on the table; talk to people instead even if for ten minutes; also, aligning my actions and thinking with the guiding principles helps me to communicate clearly."

Then he elaborated:

The other thing I learned is to be careful about my own reactions with people who have previously caused me tension or stress in interchanges ... I find that even when people

(Continued)

(Continued)

disagree vehemently and I struggle to hear them, I've been able to find some truth or some insight or some perspective that needs to be regarded. (JM)

Toward the end of the interview without any prompting on my part, Malloy launched into what I thought was a wonderful integration of joint determination and adaptive focus.

We have got to do the instructional transformation and work on our learning environments, our culture, and on the relationships at the school level because we're never going to change people's thoughts about us as a big organization unless they have a wonderful experience at school . . . if we keep thinking that transformation can happen at the system level, then all I would be doing is sending out directions, something that would never result in the improvements required. (JM)

Without using the term *adaptability* Malloy nailed it by reflecting as follows:

There haven't been major failures because [earlier in my career] I learned one major thing. Never take yourself so seriously as a senior person, always listen to your team so that you're not out there on your own thinking that everybody's with you, and be sure you're willing to change course even if you are a big complex system. My other rule of thumb is please don't laminate your improvement process and create a poster because it might be changed next month. So, our conceptual frameworks, our diagrams . . . and so forth, they've changed three or four times since I've been here, which is not always characteristic of big systems who like things to be clear and neat. That's why I don't think we've had as many failures if you will, because we've changed; we haven't been afraid to change. (JM)

Malloy couldn't resist commenting on my choice of book titles, *Nuance:*

> I get what you're saying about nuance. I mean there are 5, 10, 15 different ways to do something; depending on a particular context, it's going to have a different result. I think you're on to something really important. You actually helped me get my head around what I have been doing with everyone in TDSB. (JM)

Is the lesson that if you have nuance, you can recognize it when someone helps you uncover it? Or can anyone learn it? Get inside the process and find out.

Case Example Seven
Shattering Inequity
Robin Avelar La Salle and Ruth Johnson

As crucial as the growing problem of gross inequity is becoming, it is surprising (and demoralizing) that there are very few books about specific strategies to address inequity—*inside the process*—as I said in Chapter 1. *Shattering Inequities* by Robin Avelar La Salle and Ruth Johnson (2019) is such a book: it examines the inner workings of developing greater equity with precision and measurable outcomes. How can this be done in any situation, let alone on scale?

Addressing inequity is a nuance problem because the obvious strategies don't work: try mandating action even with corresponding support and see what uptake you get. Make it clear that the group has the flexibility to figure out a solution and you will find yourself

(Continued)

(Continued)

"waiting for Godot." Avelar La Salle and Johnson provide an alternative to this either/or alternative (imposition or laissez-faire). I have adapted the following case from one of their examples (Avelar La Salle & Johnson, 2019, Chapter 5).

The authors start with a few "have you ever wondered" questions:

- "How [do you] inspire people whose fundamental view of equity does not match yours?"
- "What do you do when you identify inequitable practices that people are completely committed to?"
- "How do you respond when people say outrageous things about vulnerable students in your presence?"
- "What is the best way to unravel inequitable practices even when you are about the only one who is concerned?"

Paradoxically, nuance leaders are often blunt about the questions. It is in the means of making progress that their appreciation of detail, discovery, and adaptability come forcefully into play. Addressing inequity is one of those confounding issues that require both bluntness and flexibility.

It was this kind of dilemma that faced Dr. Durán, a young principal in a successful K–6 school, when there was a sudden 25% influx of students moving in from another neighborhood who were decidedly unlike the students of the current population. Most of the new students were Latino and African American, and many came from low-income circumstances. At the outset the staff was a welcoming group working to embrace the new students, encouraging new families to attend school functions, and making sure to include them. It became clear fairly quickly that the new students were different: they did not have the academic background that students in the district had acquired over time. Their use of language in school and academic settings was informal. Their reading and math skills were not at level, and their writing was weak as well. In a sense we had here a welcoming staff with little idea of what they were getting into.

Later in the first year of this new scenario Dr. Durán visited a series of classrooms and had the sinking feeling that the needs of the new students were not being met. As Avelar La Salle and Johnson put it: "even equity-oriented educators do not necessarily have sufficient background and training to effectively address challenges when they find themselves immersed in troublesome situations." Dr. Durán's observations included the following:

- "New students were physically isolated."
- "Many teachers had caregiver personalities but were not necessarily models of powerful teaching and learning."
- "There was a disproportionate emphasis on school rules, pillars of good character, and other markers of student conduct."

As Avelar La Salle and Johnson note, Dr. Durán came to the conclusion that his plan for supporting the school's new students was actually bad. There was no sugarcoating it. The reader might now think that the principal should have worked with the staff in the first place to develop a plan that addressed the newcomers. This may have helped, or it could have made matters worse, given the absence of knowledge and experience about what the new situation would actually bring. And it does seem plausible that a successful school with a welcoming and caring staff would be confident that they were on the right track. Remember also that very, very few schools have figured how to be *effectively action-oriented* in the face of inequity.

In any case, Durán had a potential mess on his hands. Avela La Salle and Johnson observe, "If handled poorly, a misalignment of this sort could spin out of control and create divisiveness and infighting, the ramifications of which could last for years."

What would you do as a leader in that situation? What if it looked as if the interests of the adults were being placed ahead of the needs of the students? Or that staff actually did not know what to do, but found it difficult to admit that to themselves, let alone to others? It won't surprise you that facing seemingly unsolvable

(*Continued*)

(Continued)

problems is not that unusual when it comes to inequity. However, it may surprise you that nuance leaders (and I consider Dr. Durán to be one) facing intractable situations often do not know exactly what to do early on. This incidentally takes us back to Leonardo's mode of learning deeply that we saw in Chapter 1: "experience and experiment." You can't possibly know a given situation without getting inside it.

So, what did Durán do? Here are a few of the assumptions and corresponding actions that Durán identified for himself and conveyed to staff:

- "Presume positive intentions."
- "When you get stumped, think aloud" (when you don't know what to say, say, "I don't know what to say").
- "Try on someone else's shoes (what if you had limited content knowledge, lack of sound technical expertise, anxiety about not being able to navigate potential politics, and/or a sense of loss of some sort, e.g., power, respect, prestige, autonomy?)."

(Avelar La Salle & Johnson, Chapter 5)

Dr. Durán himself had some notion about what to do because he had been in similar situations and had equity action ideas. But he did not know how to enter into a discussion with teachers about these ideas. When he did try to explore them, teachers showed ambivalence. Here is the dilemma such a leader faces: He knows the status quo is wrong, he has some ideas about how to address it, and he realizes that he can't just tell the people what to do (being right has never been an effective strategy). Here is what he did. Somehow a wonderfully nuanced idea came to him when he said to staff in a meeting: "*I want you to want to do this.*"

Avelar La Salle and Johnson, the staff, and I as reader all had the same reaction: *What!* What the hell kind of strategy is that?

On second thought, it is not a bad way of getting out from between a rock and a hard place. The leader in a sense is saying I have some ideas; I don't know whether they are fully right; I don't expect you to accept them holus-bolus; but "I want you to want to help solve this problem."

Durán said to the staff, "Here is my initial idea: I want you to implement heterogeneous classes with strategic, differentiated, and leveled expanded day extra support." He told them that things needed to change and that his proposal was sound, so he hoped they'd want to try it. But he added the nuance that, "I want you to want to try this, but if you choose not to, then bring me an alternative proposal and we will consider it together." He added that his own proposal could be adapted as long as the basic principles stayed intact.

In short, he invited teachers to "want to want to," gave them the option to propose an alternative solution, and committed to working with them in all cases. He stated one major (and I would say nuanced) guideline:

> *Empower with clear parameters.* Why is such a stance nuanced? Because it gives direction; because it does not impose details; and because it is a beautiful example of our "trust and interact" mode of leading that I take up in Chapter 4 (the leader commits to jointly working out the details through interaction).

The three parameters that Durán set out were that any proposals

1. must give every child the best opportunity to maximize his or her learning and achievement;

2. must be grounded in research and best practice; and

3. must adhere to legal requirements.

What ensued was a new redesign with teacher feedback and ideas whereby coaching and collaborative planning time were provided. Avelar La Salle and Johnson state in that regard:

> Success was not immediate, but over the next two years, instruction for all students became visibly stronger. As a

(Continued)

(Continued)

consequence, the school culture eventually became cohesive once again, with no notable distinction between "our" students and the "new" ones, either in the classroom or in social areas of the school. And significantly, the achievement gap between the student groups was cut in half in just two years and continued to improve each year after that.

If we reflect on what Dr. Durán as a leader did, he embodies many of the qualities that I identified in Chapter 1 as characteristics of nuanced leaders. They have a commitment and a curiosity about what is possible; they are determined that the group to be successful; they connect people to the cause; and they are courageously and relentlessly committed to a better future.

Case Example Eight
Global Initiative in Deep Learning
Michael Fullan, Joanne Quinn, and Joanne McEachen

My colleagues and I have been working on deep learning since 2014. It started through the growing realization that conventionally organized schooling was no longer fit for purpose. Many studies showed that students (and their teachers) were less and less engaged as they moved up the grade levels. By Grade Ten barely more than a third of the students could be classified as engaged in their schoolwork. Or how about a rhetorical question: Is it possible for a student to get good grades all the way through and graduate and still not be good at life? What about the increasing number of students in poverty, or who didn't fit in, and thus never felt that they belonged or wanted to belong? So, the *push* of regular schools was leaning outward. We also noticed that anxiety and stress were growing rapidly and affecting everyone, children and adults alike. At the same time the *pull* of the outside increasingly global world was beckoning for better or worse. Digital attractions and distractions ran amok. I wrote a book called *Stratosphere: Integrating Technology, Pedagogy, and Change Knowledge* (Fullan, 2013a). Then I began to notice schools that were moving in the direction of integrating technology and learning, but they were few in number.

We saw this tension between irrelevance and being stymied about what to do as untenable, so we established a global initiative called *New Pedagogies for Deep Learning* (www.npdl.global). This consisted of clusters of schools (over 1,000 in total) from seven different countries that were interested in pursuing major changes in schooling that would engage students and teachers in deeper, more relevant learning experiences (Australia, Canada, Finland, Netherlands, New Zealand, Uruguay, and the United States). We provided the initial framework and supporting strategies and tools. The learning outcomes consisted of the 6Cs (character, citizenship, collaboration, communication, creativity, and critical thinking). The new pedagogy had four components (learning partnerships, pedagogical practices, learning environments, and leveraging digital). We also developed strategies related to school leadership and culture, district and local infrastructure, and system policy and resources (see Fullan, Quinn, & McEachen, 2018). NPDL represents a classic adaptive focus problem: a critical issue, lofty aspirations, broad but undeveloped ideas, innovation, and willing participants. We needed solutions but had to work them out on the ground. Our work took on the feel of a powerful social movement. We changed the name to *Deep Learning* because it was no longer a project. We have already seen one case example of districtwide deep learning in Chapter 2 from the Ottawa Catholic School Board. We pursue the concept of deep learning more broadly in this section because almost by definition its newness means that adaptability will be required.

Deep learning is quality learning that sticks with you the rest of your life; it increases student engagement through personalization and ownership; it connects students to the "real world"; it resonates

(Continued)

(Continued)

with spiritual values; it builds skills, knowledge, self-confidence, and self-efficacy; it develops new relationships with and between learners, their teachers, families and communities; and it deepens the human desire to connect with others to do good. In terms of outcomes, deep learning focuses on the 6 specific global competencies named above.

In terms of pedagogy we have built learning around four elements: learning partnerships, pedagogical practices, learning environments, and leveraging digital use. The whole set is fueled by collaborative inquiry. We have tools—ideas, rubrics, and progressions—to support development and implementation.

The other key factor for us is that we go from practice to theory. Over the past four years—with over 1,000 schools in clusters in seven countries—we have established a "living laboratory" of plan, do, reflect, extract key examples and learn; then do some more as we learn from each other and share with the world.

We are blunt in the book: "There is no reason for the majority of students to take conventional schooling seriously." This also applies to students who are doing okay on tests. Deep learning with its focus on the 6Cs produces students who are "good at life." This applies to all students, but what we started to notice was that students who are most disconnected from regular schooling are the ones who respond best to the new way. They do this because deep learning is hands-on, applied to real life, inquiry based, relevant to practical immersion and so on. This development is especially noteworthy because we did not anticipate such dramatic impact—*it emerged naturally from the work.*

Disconnected students find schooling less relevant and have little sense of belonging to a community. Moreover, their lives might be in disarray: safety, shelter, food, and health may all be problematic. Deep learning cannot do everything, but it can encompass this wider array of issues in the context of learning and development. Because deep learning is hands-on and immediately relevant to personal lives, it has a chance of developing a strong sense of efficacy, confidence, and competence. If deep learning can help disconnected students come out of the rut they find themselves in, they can actually "take off" more than other students. Beyond their own situation, such students come to see their own worth and their ability to contribute to the world. Peers and teachers notice that they contribute and find their place. We have many examples in the book of students who experienced such transformation. The bigger point is that *all students gain.* In a real sense we think that deep learning has a chance to help reduce inequity in education, which, as we know, is an ever-increasing trend with dangerous consequences for society as well as for individuals.

Finally, it is important to note that our work focused on the *public education system.* There are few things as crucial and as potentially uplifting as transforming the current system. In the deep learning work all teachers (or rather every group of teachers and schools) find their own entry point as they interact with us and other schools in cluster-related development. Many teachers would begin by giving students greater voice and choice and ways in which you can increase student choice and voice. Once we give students more choice and voice, it naturally leads to greater communication and collaboration between and among students and teachers. Next, teachers tend to think about the learning environment and how to be more intentional in learning designs that foster deep learning (the development of the global competencies). The explicitness of the tools supports teachers in each step and builds clarity and precision.

More detail about our first three years in DL is provided in our book *Deep Learning: Engage the World Change the World* (Fullan, Quinn, & McEachen, 2018), so we just concentrate on nuance here. In this initiative there was much evidence of joint determination, as we had to work out common and unique details in seven different cultures and countries, as well as many local variations. As for the theme of this chapter, there have been several fundamental discoveries that I would attribute to adaptability. I cite here four big ones: students as

(Continued)

(Continued)

change agents, the equity hypothesis, the matter of catalytic Cs (where certain Cs cause others to be pursued simultaneously), and the theme of engage the world. We had none of these ideas in our original design.

First, we saw time and again that students and children were natural change agents. They have no particular commitment to the status quo, have a propensity for helping humanity, and are action oriented with a sense of immediacy. We have not found a child young enough who, if given the opportunity, is not inclined to act on improving the situation. For example, there was the 10-year-old girl from Uruguay who said in Spanish, "I am supposed to help humanity so I decided to start with my own neighborhood." She promptly got together with a small group and designed a robot that vibrated and scared off birds when they flew too close to the vegetable garden that they had previously been raiding.

The equity hypothesis is another powerful discovery. We noticed that DL was good for all students but was especially powerful for students who were disconnected from schooling. Instead of saddling them with remedial work that added insult to injury, personally meaningful learning that had a practical application and involved a few peers really turned them on. We coined the phrase *Don't dumb down; smarten up.* We are now developing specific DL strategies that are aimed at marginal students and that should lead to whole new approaches to students alienated from regular schooling—a theme I return to in Chapter 5.

> Deep learning is good for all students, but especially powerful for students who are disconnected from schooling.

Third, we found that two of the Cs—character and citizenship—are catalytic: if you focus on one or both, they ramify through the other Cs. Prior to our work, four of the Cs had been around for 25 or so years and had been ignored (the so-called 21st century skills: collaboration, communication, creativity, and crucial thinking). In addition, the much-neglected phenomenon of creativity can be catalytic for students in that those who are alienated or bored with conventional schooling can be transformed if they get a chance to invent or adapt new ideas and things. Creativity, as we know from Sir Ken Robinson's more than three decades of making the case, has been the neglected child of 21st century skills to the detriment of students and society alike (Robinson, 2018). With deep learning, the 6Cs, and knowledge of system change, we are now in a position to bring creativity front and center as a catalytic C that will revamp the learning of students and teachers and will potentially radically alter learning. Incidentally, if you are one of the millions of people who have heard Sir Ken speak, you will know that he is a master of nuance (or is it irony, or both?).

Fourth, the core purpose of education became revealed. It took us back to Brazilian educator and philosopher Paulo Freire, who said that the fundamental purpose of education was "to act upon and transform the world [in order to] move towards ever new possibilities of a fuller and richer life individually and collectively" (2000, p. 32). Students, if stimulated and given the opportunity, did want to engage with the world, learn more, and change things for the better. Given the state of the world, they did not want to wait to become citizens 10 years from now; they wanted to be connected today—not a moment to spare. All of this comes from immersion in detail as it links upward to an overriding purpose—in this case fostering deep learning.

ADAPTABILITY

Joint determination and adaptability are seamless. These two aspects of nuance take us into detail where we don't find weeds but rather leaders who help identify and develop patterns that enable us to decipher the trees, while we increasingly see the forest. Detail is essential, as Leonardo proved instinctively and experientially time and again. His learning motto, as you may recall from Chapter 1, was "experience and experiment." See the detail, note the connections, see the system at work, and then experiment further to see what more can be done with the insight. This is exactly our experience with the equity hypothesis. We noticed that some previously distant students were becoming engaged. We saw why citizenship and character were alluring. We found that creativity, innovation, and entrepreneurship unleashed brilliant new ideas and energy from some students who hitherto were passive. We speculated that becoming more explicit would be a good experiment. We are now testing the new theory in our work to see if we can prove the equity hypothesis and foster the spread of practices that will radically reduce inequity in public education.

In all of this, leaders *learn and lead* in equal measure. They help scores of others do the same. This is the deep meaning of learning systems. They are stocked with people who see new learning as the norm, who know that you can't lead without learning, and who seek breakthroughs by mobilizing these capacities in others.

The reader who wants greater nuance doesn't have to understand the detailed theory, but rather to become proficient in joint determination (being right at the end of the meeting), and adaptability (learn and lead). Guiding principles and learning-oriented experience are a two-way street. They feed on each other, which is essential to the adaptive processes and resolution. Roger Martin and Sally Osberg capture this "learn and lead" principle wonderfully in their examination of successful system-level social entrepreneurship that addressed intractable problems such as abject poverty. They call this phenomenon, *expertise and apprenticeship*—be a good expert on what you know but also learn from others about what you don't know (the apprentice):

> The social entrepreneur [any top leader in our terms] will also learn to draw on the wisdom of those not classified as experts, especially those living within the system in order to gain insights about their beliefs and practices. Instead of deferring to the prevailing wisdom of those who benefit from the status quo, [position yourself] to absorb lessons from ecosystem actors, especially those disadvantaged by the existing equilibrium. (Martin & Osberg, 2015, p. 92)

This of course is nuance—deliberately seeking insight from not-so-obvious places. In short, adaptability subjects one's values and principles to a reality test whereby your stance as a learner enables you to test and refine what you know, indeed, to learn completely new things. You shift course based on what you are learning. You then focus with renewed accuracy as you and the group push to new levels of accomplishment. You are confident enough to be an expert about things you know, but humble enough to be an apprentice when you have something to learn from others. You are a learner and leader who commands respect because you listen, have good ideas, are willing to recalibrate, and learn to act by acting to learn.

4

culture-based accountability

trust and interact

Accountability has been the bugbear of human systems for millennia. In education it has played a particularly ignominious role in the history of reform. Two of my favorite nuanced colleagues—Tim Brighouse and Viviane Robinson—have captured each side of the dilemma when they reacted to this chapter. One horn of the dilemma is that sometimes "the system" is so punitive and demanding that it is the leader's job to protect schools from external interventions that do more harm than good. In the 1990s Tim was the CEO of Birmingham's Local Education Authority

(LEA), which had over 500 schools. He became infamous for suing his own minister of education, who made the mistake of sitting beside an open microphone and commenting on Tim's selection as director by saying, "Why did they appoint that nutter?" Tim sued the minister and eventually settled out of court for a tidy sum. He promptly created an innovation fund and named it after the minister. Touché! Tim also led "The London Challenge," which changed the quality and reputation of teachers in greater London, which has a workforce of over 60,000 teachers. When Tim read my argument for what I was calling "natural accountability" within the culture, he responded with these words:

> I saw my role at the LEA level—as it was then—to work like mad to protect the schools from the climate being set by central government, which had a habit of sending thunderbolts of disruption. (Sometimes I called it creating a kind of umbrella against the storms of national prescription). I think "nuance" requires leaders to be deeply conscious of the need to "affect" climate at every level. That's why communication is so important. So I saw my role as visiting schools non-stop, sending thousands of personal follow-up cards/letters of thanks, and further enquiry—it was a pre-digital age—and making sure other members of staff were regularly telling me of examples of staff commitment so I could re-enforce with follow-up unexpected letters telling the person how the other colleague had been praising them. (personal communication, May 2018)

Tim's position was that the external system was so arbitrary that it had to be thwarted. Viviane Robinson, on the other hand, reminds us of the history of the teaching profession. It has been marked by privacy of the classroom and isolation of teachers from each other. Whatever you think of individual teacher autonomy, day-to-day accountability is not its strong suit. Thus, Robinson worries about how to coordinate loosely coupled work. In her words:

> The coordination and accountability that comes from that approach [Leaving accountability to local culture] is likely to be much weaker in education than in some other fields where the technology is so much more standardised and well developed. The enormous variation in how work is done allows multiple approaches

and standards, and a team will need deliberate social interventions to arrive at truly joint work. The interpersonal dynamics and capabilities are central here. Rather than produce joint accountability, some teams spend most of their time in parallel play. (personal communication, June 2018)

We have already seen Robinson's solution in Chapter 2 with respect to the process of double loop learning, which uncovers factors that get at root causes. This dilemma—if you intervene in a ham-handed way, you make matters worse vs. if you leave situation be, things will stagnate and fail to improve—has plagued education reform throughout the modern era of reform over the past half century. Jal Mehta (2013) captures this phenomenon eloquently in his book *The Allure of Order* when he observes: "We increase external pressure and accountability, hoping we can do on the back end what we failed to create on the front-end" [build a high capacity teaching force] (p. 7). Well, we are at the back end, so what do we do? Let's build the argument.

I start with a definition of "culture-based accountability." Essentially, it is individual and collective responsibility that becomes embedded into the values, behavior, and actions of people in the situation. It is specific, transparent, and evidence based. People in the culture come to embrace a focus on continuous improvement as something they have to do and prove to themselves and to others. As culture-based accountability develops, it engages external assessment as part of its responsibility. Let's examine how it works.

First, we will revisit why traditional approaches to accountability don't work. Then I will lay out the basis for "culture-based accountability" based on what I call "six sticky phrases." The third section provides two examples of natural accountability in action—a state in Australia, and a school district in California. As usual, we end up with nuanced strategies that galvanize groups.

THE FRUITLESS PURSUIT OF TOP-DOWN ACCOUNTABILITY

The flip side of nuance in the face of complex problems is failure. Surfacers are in a hurry. They want quick results via direct action. Recall my drivers reference, in which I portrayed four wrong drivers for whole system reform

(Fullan, 2011): accountability, individualism, technology, and ad hoc policies. A driver is a policy; a wrong driver is one that does not work. Direct accountability—a carrots-and-stick approach—does not work because it is imposed on the people affected by it who have little say in the matter. Daniel Koretz, an expert in assessment and testing, documents in agonizing detail what he calls *The Testing Charade* (2017). With documentation to spare, Koretz describes that high-stakes testing leads to score inflation, cheating on the part of top officials, bad test prep, making up unrealistic targets, invalid and unreliable evaluation of teachers, and no evidence that kids learn more. When the system turns bad, it's human nature for some people to game an imposed high-stakes system, not to mention that it fundamentally violates our first two nuance principles: joint determination and adaptability.

Second, there are several other weak approaches to accountability that stand out: performance appraisal, professional development training, standards, and professional learning communities. This set represents a mixture of either dysfunctional and/or weak interventions for bringing about change. The main problem with these strategies is that they are used in a literal—one could say non-nuanced—manner and, as such, become inevitably superficial and counterproductive. My point is not that they are useless (although they can be), but that they are not powerful enough to make a big difference in system performance.

First, performance appraisal (often connected to some form of merit pay) has remained in the category of what Pfeffer and Sutton (2006) called "dangerous half-truths and total nonsense." In later work, Sutton and Rao (2014) definitively dispose of performance appraisal by quoting W. Edwards Deming, and then draw on the experience of Adobe Systems, the modern-day multinational software giant. Deming declared that performance reviews "[foster] short-term performance, annihilate long-term planning, build fear, demolish teamwork, nourish rivalry and politics" (quoted in Sutton & Rao, 2014, p. 112). Sutton and Rao then quote an internal study from Adobe:

> [The internal research team] calculated that annual reviews required 80,000 hours of time from the 2,000 managers at Adobe each year, the equivalent of 40 full-time employees. After all that effort, internal surveys revealed that employees felt less inspired and motivated afterwards—and turnover increased. (p. 113)

Business professor Jody Gittell has spent a couple of decades investigating the relationship between relational coordination and performance in the airline industry and in the hospital sector. Her main finding is that in most organizations supervisors spend counterproductive time in superficial reviews and in trying to find out what went wrong so that they can lay blame to pressure workers to improve performance. In low performing organizations Gittell found that

> instead of building shared goals with employees, working side by side with them and providing coaching and feedback, supervisors spent their limited time communicating performance standards and measuring performance. (Gittell, 2016, p. 46)

As one supervisor in an ineffective organization stated, "We only have time to focus on the bad apples" (p. 46).

By contrast, in the high performing organizations supervisors were observed spending more time coaching and giving workers feedback that "took the form of problem solving and advising, rather than assessing compliance with performance objectives" (p. 48). Shortly we will see how Jim Watterston, director general of the sprawling Queensland, Australia, school system, with 1,200 schools spread over 7,000 kilometers and 86,000 employees, designed just such a system with great results.

Want more? Try Tamra Chandler's (2016) *How Performance Management Is Killing Performance.* In short, performance appraisal is episodic, very few are good at it, and above all, it is an extremely weak intervention for changing people's behavior. It can be of some value for induction or other forms of supporting beginners, but is, at best, a waste of time for ongoing learning. It is simply not strong enough to affect practice.

Performance appraisal is episodic, very few are good at it, and, above all, it is an extremely weak intervention for changing people's behavior.

Professional development and training obviously can be of some value, but my question is, How powerful is it for changing beliefs and practice? Most direct training does not end up changing practice because it is used by "surfacers" to attempt to get direct results with ad hoc means. Load up on training and expect the results to follow. Professional standards are in the same category. Focus directly on the standards and the organization will improve. Standards per se cannot serve as a direct means of changing cultures. To be effective they must be used as catalysts for changing culture.

One more popular bromide is professional learning communities (PLCs). Superficiality is the mark of leaders who want quick fixes. This is why the report *Teachers Know Best* (Boston Consulting Group, 2014), funded by the Gates Foundation, came up with a rather curious finding. It found that administrators liked PLCS more than teachers did, yet teachers said they valued professional learning that favored "focused teamwork, shared instructional planning and assessment, and a positive culture"—the very characteristics of good PLCS. What explains this apparent contradiction? The answer: PLCs were run too much by administrators and were not jointly determined with teachers around factors related to deeper change.

I like good PLCs. I value professional standards such as those from the Australian Institute for Teaching for School Leadership (2017), Learning Forward (2017), a U.S.-based professional association devoted to professional and student learning, and the government of Alberta (2018), but my overall point is that professional standards by themselves are not frequent enough or strong enough to carry the day.

So, what *is* the solution? Richard Elmore pointed us in the right direction in 2004 when he drew this conclusion: "no amount of external accountability will be effective in the absence of internal accountability." The latter concerns accountability that is built into the culture of the organization. It stems from the nature of nuanced but nonetheless explicit actions that, for example, are embedded in the cultures of the cases we have been examining, such as Malloy in TDSB and Bretherton in Benjamin Adlard. Let's examine the argument in more detail.

INGREDIENTS OF CULTURE-BASED ACCOUNTABILITY

In our day-to-day work in school systems, we drew the conclusion that 80% of the best change ideas came from leading practitioners rather than research per se. This is because the best ideas are detailed ones that get at, if you like, the nuances of change dynamics. I have come to call these practical insights "sticky phrases"—insights that once you identify them as memorable concepts, they stay with you. Figure 4.1 contains our most powerful findings—ones that are subtle and are reflective of strong cultures. I first define them and then pick them up in two case examples. By the way, these six insights interact in mutually reinforcing ways.

Figure 4.1 Sticky Change Phrases

1. Use the group to change the group

2. Precision over prescription

3. Feedback: collaboration, candor, and autonomy

4. Trust and interact vs. trust but verify

5. See the forest and the trees

6. Accountability as culture

1. Use the Group to Change the Group

The opposite of nuance is directness. One such example in school leadership is cited by Macbeath and his colleagues (2018) in referring to "the most improved school in England" from a case study conducted by Mary James:

> The success of the school was owed to the uncompromising headteacher who was not hesitant in claiming ownership of policy and strategy . . . He is quoted as saying "This policy has got a lot of me in it. It's largely me" and "that wasn't from staff. That was from myself . . . I think teachers have got to feel that they're making decisions, but I suppose [what] I am forcing them to do is to make those decisions." (pp. 9–10)

Not an ounce of nuance, yet evidently successful in raising achievement scores. It doesn't take a genius to know that not much will continue after this head leaves his school. By contrast, the school leader who develops the group while she or he leads has long lasting impact and must lead with subtlety, especially at the beginning. We saw this clearly in the case of executive head teacher Bretherton in Chapter 2.

We also see the nature and the power of this kind of leadership in Viviane Robinson's (2011) findings when she identified the most powerful school leadership factors associated with increased student achievement. At the top of the list by a large margin was: "Leading, teaching, learning, and development." As we put it in our own work, the most effective principal is the one who "participates as a learner" working alongside teachers in moving the school forward. Several things happen simultaneously: the principal actually *learns* more and more; he or she does not have to be the best pedagogue in the building but does need to know about developing and leading pedagogues; the leader creates a climate for all to learn including herself or himself; the leader enables others to grow to the point where there are many teacher leaders. The final effect is that the principal as lead learner influences teacher development indirectly, *but nonetheless explicitly* in moving the school forward. Using the group to change the group is nuance. More gets done in the short run, while in-built capacity provides lasting benefit. Finally and quite explicitly, the culture of the school changes for the better as the group increases its capacity to learn and be responsible together.

2. Precision Over Prescription

Nuance leaders are famous for resolving dilemmas. Surfacers choose one side of the dilemma or the other. Some want change fast so they prescribe (and fail). Others don't have the confidence to impose so they leave it open ended (and fail). The answer is neither imposition nor laissez-faire work. The trick is to foster precision by leading the exploration of the problem, enabling the volunteerism and ideas of individuals and the group, including the leader, to help solve most of the difficulties. The leader can still be insistent to a point, but stop short of imposition. Precision is more powerful than command.

Leaders with nuance know how to get at precision without imposition. Probably vagueness is more of a problem than overspecification. In our own work we undertake to discover and formulate the causal pathways to measurable student outcomes, not because we want to please the accountability system but rather because we want to have an impact. With good precision, as colleagues work on and solve problems or implement new practices that work, you don't have to impose the solutions. There is a ready acceptance of ideas that work when they are co-discovered. Normally you don't have to impose something that works if it has been developed in practice with your peers.

One of W. Edwards Deming's core ideas about "profound knowledge" was "understanding variation." You can never know what causes something until you get inside the process in the particular situation. Leonardo, as we have seen, was a master at examining detail for the purpose of sorting out what made something tick. Tony Bryk and his team identify variation in performance as one of six key components of their science of improvement:

> Achieving improvements at scale is not about what works on the average. It is about getting quality results under a variety of conditions. Understanding the sources of variation in outcomes, and responding effectively to them, lies at the heart of quality improvement. (Bryk et al., 2015, p. 35)

In the previous section I talked about the importance of school leaders participating as learners. One of the main reasons for following this practice is so they can see specificity firsthand. The critical importance of doing this can be seen in a piece of research on eight middle schools in two districts with comparable demographics that all were engaged in implementing PLCS. The findings for the eight schools in the two districts were similar in terms of teacher survey responses to such items as "agreement about the need to collaborate" and about "what should be a learning community." But when it came to details, there were significant differences—particularly when it involved making specific links to student learning. There were major differences on questions pertaining to whether "teachers examine and compare student learning results," "teachers discuss instructional methods used to teach students," and "seek new teaching methods, testing and reflecting on results." The four schools in District A had mean score responses on these questions on a five-point scale in the 2.17 to 2.44 range, whereas District B responses were in the 3.19 to 3.70 range (Wells & Feun, 2013). District B showed evidence of increased student achievement; District A did not. Implementing specific actions known to affect learning made the difference. Specificity matters. It would be a fundamental change error to take these specifics and prescribe them for other schools. Precision requires process, not a checklist. It is when the group, well led, works through the issues, gets skilled at the particular actions, sees the results and builds on them that the results start to accumulate. In this process people become committed to doing what is effective because they see how it works up close.

In sum, the vast majority of people will do the (accountable) right thing when they are part of a collective specification process. It goes nowhere or wrong only when it either remains vague or becomes imposed through surveillance. I will return to the question of variation at the end of this chapter. To put the question in accountability terms: how do you reduce bad variation, i.e., variation in effectiveness? Culture-based accountability does just that.

3. Feedback: Collaboration, Candor, and Autonomy

Good feedback is one of the cornerstones of individual and group growth. Humans want feedback in general, but not in specific (unless it is praise!). Accountability in principle is supposed to give good feedback in order to improve things, but it flounders as a top-down phenomenon because those above us are frequently not good at giving feedback, knowledgeable enough, or trusted. Feedback is vital for actual improvement, not just mere change, to use Viviane Robinson's (2018) key distinction. Because quality feedback enters the arena of necessary change, it is going to have to be finessed to be effective. It is in other words going to require leaders who know nuance. We will meet several such leaders in this chapter, but let's start with Ed Catmull.

Catmull is the CEO and president of Pixar Animation. In his book *Creativity Inc.*, a big question that he takes up is how Pixar was able to make 14 (and still counting) blockbuster animated movies in a row (starting with *Toy Story)* in a highly competitive industry. Catmull (2014) seems to be rare among CEOs in his preoccupation with what makes an effective organization. In tackling this problem—in effect setting up his own feedback system—he learned a great deal about the nature of highly creative organizations:

> I've spent nearly forty years thinking about how to help smart, ambitious people work effectively with one another . . . I believe that managers must loosen controls, not tighten them. They must accept risk; they must trust people they work with and strive to clear the path for them, and always they must pay attention to and engage anything that creates fear. (pp. xv–xvi)

What Catmull also had to do was to figure out how to establish a culture that both valued autonomy and supplied valuable feedback that would be acted on. In fact, he combined "candor and autonomy." To do this Pixar established a group it called the *Braintrust*—a group of peers who met every few months or so to assess and give feedback to the movie director as a film is being made. As Catmull (2015, p. 87) put it: "Put smart, passionate people in a room together, and charge them with identifying and solving problems, and encourage them to be candid with each other." In any complex endeavor, early versions will almost certainly be deficient in some ways. This is normal. Feedback is fortune because it is essential for improvement, especially in the early phases of the work when things have not been fully worked out.

But how do you get people to take the feedback seriously? Paradoxically, autonomy—the norm that the receiver has the right to reject the advice—is the condition that makes the advice more likely to be taken seriously. Catmul explains:

> The Braintrust watches early mock ups of the movie and discusses what is not ringing true, what could be better, what's not working at all. Notably, they do not *prescribe* how to fix the problems they diagnose. They test weak points, they make suggestions, but it is up to the director to settle on the path forward. (p. 90, italics in the original)

Catmull says that the Braintrust doesn't *want* to solve the problem, because it is likely that director and his or her creative team will come up with a better solution, once they get good feedback. This reminds me of Tim Brighouse, whom I introduced at the beginning of this chapter:

> I have always made the point with school leaders that the great danger for leaders is that they overdo the "answers" and neglect the "questions." So those for whom the leader is responsible are inclined to seek permission or require advice on how to solve the problem and the easiest—but often the worst—thing the leader can do is provide the answer. So, I believe the skill of the "nuance" leader is to ask questions rather than supply answers. That's not to say that they never have to provide the answer, but it shouldn't be their default position. Connected with that is the need for them to

always think aloud or "speculate" to encourage exploration of the issue. (personal communication, May 2018)

We saw this habit of reflective pursuit of complex questions with John Malloy and Dr. Durán in Chapter 3 and will see a further example with Jim Watterston later in this chapter. The larger the organization and the more complex the problem, the more you need a culture of continuous probing and related problem resolution.

Back to Pixar. Autonomy and collaboration are not mutually exclusive. When you combine candor, autonomy, and collaboration, this is what you get: First, autonomy is not isolation. Prolonged isolation is unhealthy whether you are an individual or a group. You simply may not grow and will certainly deteriorate over time. If you are part of a group who respects your autonomy, you will receive good ideas, develop your own versions, and bring them back to the group. The group will respect individual autonomy but also work out joint solutions that will benefit all. This is what Andy Hargreaves and I call *Collaborative Professionalism* (Fullan & Hargreaves, 2016; Hargreaves & O'Connor, 2018). Collaborative professionalism respects autonomy and collaboration in combination in the service of deep change that affects students with better learning and radically reduced inequity. All of my case examples in this book reflect this quality. The result is natural accountability that becomes embedded into the culture of the system.

4. Trust and Interact vs. Trust but Verify

This is pure nuance territory. In the 1980s when President Ronald Reagan was dealing with Mikhail Gorbachev of Russia, he was advised by his Russian tutor to throw in a Russian proverb or two. One such was *trust but verify*. When you look closely, it is not trust at all because it requires extensive and continuous verification from both sides to monitor compliance. In 2013, Secretary of State John Kerry stated more accurately, "verify and verify." No nuance there. If it is a life-and-death situation, fair enough—trust and be vigilant. Or better still, just be vigilant.

On the other hand, if you are trying to build something new, including commitments and breakthrough success, you'd better take a different stance. If leaders believe that followers first have to earn trust, they actually will foster mistrust. You have to invest in trust *before* people have earned it. Trust is a verb before it becomes a state. If you have to verify everything, you might as well not call it trust. Just mainline verification. This is what hardline accountability leaders do. Of course, it doesn't work except under certain conditions. If the desired behavior doesn't require any skill (such as wearing seatbelts or not trespassing in restricted areas), you achieve the desired outcome with strong surveillance. But if the outcome involves new capacities, commitment beyond the minimum, innovation, helping others, and so on, building trust for the long term is required.

Trust *and* interaction together is the nuance. When we found that leaders who participate as learners are more successful, it was not only because they were learning how to become more effective, but also because they were part and parcel of a process that sorted out what was working or not. Once leaders become dependable as trustworthy and interactive partners, they become part of the group. They don't have to be present all the time for group trust (autonomy and candor) to flourish. They have created a culture whereby specific interaction *is* accountability. The leader has solved most of the accountability problems *naturally,* i.e., within the culture itself. External assessment data are still used but more openly and more in control of those inside because the insiders are using the external data along with internal assessments. Effective organizations don't passively follow state directives and data, but rather proactively consume the information at hand. Leaders who trust and interact are more likely to catch problems earlier and more likely to be able to take decisive action when needed (the group, if you like, allows or even supports strong action under these conditions).

Such internal accountability combined with external accountability data (not the other way around) provides greater coherence to the work and greater performance (Fullan & Quinn, 2016, Chapter 5). The nuance is inside the process while the benefits accrue both inside and outside.

5. See the Forest and the Trees

As we saw with Leonardo when he went into detail (such as dissecting corpses to trace how certain muscles might expand and contract), he did not get lost in the weeds, but rather used it as input to understand the bigger entity. The previous four "sticky" processes in action enable our leader to be constantly schooled in the detail of change. In our evolving work we have also seen and helped develop leaders connect to the bigger picture. They become proactive consumers of external ideas.

In his decades long work identifying competencies of especially effective leaders, Lyle Kirtman found that school leaders who focus on learning inside the school, but don't get out much, do less well on influencing student learning than leaders who pay attention inside while also linking to the outside. He describes the competency this way:

Builds External Networks and Partnerships

- Sees his or her role as a leader in a broad manner that extends outside the school
- Understands his or her role as being part of a variety of external networks
- Has a strong ability to engage people inside and outside the school setting in two-way partnerships
- Uses technology to expand and manage a network of resources people (Kirtman & Fullan, 2016, p. 15)

Andy Hargreaves and Dennis Shirley (2018) found that "leading from the middle" (LfM) benefits one's own organization and helps the larger system. LfM in this case involves leading as part of school and district or other regional networks with the purpose of widening the source of ideas and impact on multiple schools and districts. In so doing, leaders broaden their scope of learning and impact and become better partners upward to policymakers and downward to individual schools and communities. The result is that these leaders come to "See the system that produces the current outcomes"—one of Tony Bryk et al.'s (2015) core factors in the science of improvement at scale.

Given that leaders are plugged into their own organizations as I have been describing in this chapter, they "feed and are fed by" the larger system if they also participate in wider networks. With technology and a sense of purpose, it is easier to access the wider world of ideas and actions. Over time they begin to grasp the big picture, the smaller picture, and their interconnections. They don't see trees; they see patterns. They don't see abstractions; they see consequences affecting people on the ground. Looking at the same picture, nuanced leaders literally see more than other leaders even when they can't explain how they know. But I think we can explain how they *got to know*—by doing the things that I have been describing in this book: getting better at joint determination, practicing adaptability, and cultivating cultures of natural accountability. The outcome—better performance in complex environments—is predictable if not traceable in detail.

6. Accountability as Culture

What I have been describing throughout this book is new, more specific, and more purposeful patterns of interaction. They represent the day-to-day work of individuals and groups. They consist of transparent interactions aimed at measurable processes and outcomes. Most of the assessment is a function of interaction, specificity, and relative nonjudgmentalism—or to put it differently, most of the judgment is built into the interaction and its results. External accountability policies don't work because they are distant and episodic. Internal accountability is effective because it is part of the daily culture. Richard Elmore, as I mentioned, first identified this phenomenon in 2004.

> Investments in internal accountability *must logically precede* any expectation that schools will respond productively to external pressure for performance. (Elmore, 2004, p. 134, italics added)

In our book *Coherence* we defined coherence as "the shared depth of understanding of the nature of the work." Shared depth is tantamount to solid accountability through daily interaction. Accountability is on-the-spot assessment and reaction. No matter how you view accountability, daily interaction is the best form of being held responsible. When it is frequent, continuous, and transparent, you can't—nor do you want to—avoid it. Accountability is something like 80% daily culture and 20% external backup or intervention. Orchestrating this is the nuanced leader. It is natural because it is organic to the culture; it is built in, ready to be reinforced by external accountability.

It is natural because it is organic to the culture. Time to look at some concrete examples.

EXAMPLES OF NATURAL ACCOUNTABILITY
LINKED TO RESULTS

External accountability acting on its own has a poor track record. Nuanced leaders with their focus clearly centered on culture-based accountability represent a different story. Let's take two examples.

Case Example Nine
Strengthening Whole System Accountability
Queensland, Australia

What if you had just been appointed director general (DG) of education for the Australian state of Queensland—the highest-ranking civil servant in the state? The state was among the lowest performing states in the country; only the Northern Territory had lower achievement. Queensland is almost 7,000 kilometers long, has vast outback territory to the west, and many remote areas to the north. Many schools are in isolated areas. You have 1,239 schools in seven regions with each region traditionally run as separate fiefdoms. There are 86,000 people in your employ. Your bosses (the politicians and the public) want results; your followers (86,000 regional school people) want to be treated fairly. You are accountable for achieving new levels of performance within four years while pleasing all levels of the system. You already know that heavy-handed accountability won't work, but neither will a big vision backed up only by "general" encouragement. That was the situation facing Jim Watterston in 2013. What you need to do is develop what I have been calling in this chapter a culture of accountability—one that, in fact, does not exist in a system that has had silos and fiefdoms for decades.

I had worked as advisor to Watterston in 2008 when he was director general of the Australian Capital Territory in Canberra, which contained a mere 84 schools, and wrote about him in my book *Motion*

Leadership in Action (Fullan, 2013b). I had also been working with many of his schools and leaders in Queensland at different levels over the past five years. Watterston figured out his own strategies, but he drew a lot on us and on many others. I had a chance to interview him on April 4, 2017, about his first four years as DG in Queensland. I knew he had great finesse with large-scale change, and I wanted to dig deeper. The following paragraphs came from this interview.

> When I arrived, people were ready for change. They didn't know what change they wanted, but they were certainly disappointed about being castigated, if you like, for the previous six years about their performance on the national testing. It was a system where people felt like they deserved more recognition, but they didn't know how to get it. I saw my job as helping to establish enabling conditions.

Watterston first worked on what he called alignment of roles, actions, and outcomes, broadly, but not specifically setting the direction. Reminiscent of what John Malloy found when he arrived at the Toronto School District, Watterston describes the culture that he encountered at the outset:

> People were used to getting the DG's newsletter every fortnight and seeing what they had to do. Literally, it was a newsletter. This is what our priorities are; this is what is happening. So, people were hand-to-mouth fed. So, I turned the triangle upside down. I put teachers and principals at the top and me, as DG, at the bottom. I used this image for presentation in the first two years. My job was to make sure there was a structure and a strategy, but at the end of the day it is teachers and school leaders who have to do the job. So, empowerment was a big enabler. Empowerment was making sure that every person can do the job the way they think is best to bring about the outcome. But we were clear about the

(Continued)

(Continued)

outcome [improved teaching and learning linked to student results]. Where I think autonomy and empowerment get mixed up is, when autonomy is seen as "Well, I can do the job my way and I'll just hide in my space and take it away and do it." This was nothing like that. This was about making sure that as you get the alignment right, the DG works with the Deputy Director, and all the way through the system, and so the assistant regional directors are the ones who work with the principals.

In this last passage Watterston touched on several themes I have been discussing in this chapter: autonomy does not mean isolation; it means trust and interaction. Interact with others in your line of authority, but don't do their job for them. Watterston elaborates on the last point (shades of Brighouse: don't provide the answers; ask the right questions and support):

The reason we got the alignment and empowerment to go together was so the 45 assistant regional directors wouldn't feel they were the principals' bosses. They couldn't do the principals' job for them—and this was a massive culture change. We had to teach the assistant regional directors to go in and support and mentor and challenge principals, but don't do their job. So, the empowerment piece is that principals get to decide what their strategy is and how it works. Not all principals are capable of doing that.

Note the nuance. When you are knowledgeable and you interact with someone who reports to you, it is hard not to tell them what to do. But providing directives is exactly what Watterston was trying to minimize (as were Brighouse and Malloy). The nature of the interaction should help but not order people what to do. Progress is made when people learn to become more effective, figuring it out through feedback: candor, collaboration, and autonomy.

For this to work, a third (alignment and empowerment were the first two) enabler consisted of what Watterston called "capability building":

> We've got 1,239 schools across Queensland. In some places like far remote community schools it's hard to get a principal, so you don't get the best principal in those schools. You can do one of two things: you can either sack them and hope for a better replacement, or you can build their capability. There is really only one answer because if everyone is fearful for their job they would always be worried that if they did something wrong, they would be punished. So, we had to take the pressure off. But there is no point empowering principals if they don't know what to do. So, we had to re-skill assistant regional directors to teach them how to coach, to teach them how to mentor, and what to mentor them in. We had to make sure that the strategy was clear about what we wanted principals to look for, and we are still working on this after four years.

What Watterston and his team are doing is increasing the specificity of the strategy while steadfastly avoiding prescription. The fourth element identified by Watterston is at the heart of this chapter: how to handle accountability itself. The system he inherited had the trappings of accountability but not the substance:

> They had a framework that has eight elements that [were] used to conduct a teaching and learning audit. The so-called experts would go into a school and do a teaching and learning review where they would look for all the elements that they thought constitute good teaching and learning, and people would get these reports back and say "oh yeah, you've got all the elements of pedagogy." When I first arrived, I was in a school and they showed me their audit report and it

(Continued)

(Continued)

> was perfect. Everything was green. When I went back to the office, I pulled all their data and everything was red. They were being told they were great, but they weren't. The inputs didn't match the outputs.

In response, Watterston made dramatic changes and developed a new unit and process that essentially encompassed what we have been discussing this whole chapter: greater precision, causal links to outcomes, trust and interaction, transparency, nonjudgmental feedback, and autonomy for action.

> We developed what we call the school improvement unit: brand new unit. We used the same tools—we didn't have to change the framework; we wanted people to be comfortable with it. We developed external review teams who answered just to me (the DG). Accountability is the most difficult concept for a school system to absorb. We made it very clear that the idea that you could get your head chopped off in Queensland wouldn't apply. There was no mark on it. There was no red, green, or amber. There was no A–E grade or anything. All you were going to get back was recommendations for you to consider. The school improvement unit was well resourced. For every school that got its review, they had external peer reviewers (other principals) and outside consultants. So far, we have trained 1200 principals to be peer reviewers and we will get to the other 139 in a few weeks.

> These reviews are about three or four days with a minimum of three or four people. They interview everyone. They put an ad in the local newspaper and they bring in community members. It took a long time for principals to become comfortable with that because they didn't want people who might be critical of the school to come in, but these are exactly the kind of people we wanted to tag.

Then we gave back evidence-based recommendations: Here's what we saw and heard, and here's the recommendations. But they weren't "you have to go and implement this program or have to do this." The really difficult part was we kept the assistant regional directors out of the process—those people who were line mentors to the principals. There was a lot of anger in the system when we set this up, but we wanted it to be external. Then after the review was finished and the report came back, the assistant regional director came in and worked with the principal, so the two of them could build this guiding coalition within the school about what to do. It's taken a long time to embed—we're in our third year. We do 400 reviews a year. We provide an annual report that's about 200 pages, but it's not a report on how many schools we reviewed; it's about "here's what we found." In exit surveys we have found a 95% acceptance rate. The accountability piece is getting better and better. We are turning up the temperature slowly, but I would be quite absolutely certain, and very confident, that people don't fear it. In every other system I have worked in, everyone fears the inspector coming in to check you out. I think people see our review as a proactive opportunity.

Early in the above quote Watterston states "we used the same tools." So often two leaders using the exact same framework fail or succeed depending on their mindset—mindset as nuance. A fool with a tool is still a fool; a nuancer with a tool is a catalyzer of change in culture.

The final component that Watterston talked about is collaboration. He talked about the importance of each school having a game plan and for schools to learn from each other's game plan:

Collaboration applies just as much to learning around leaders. The visits I have now, I get 8–10 people talking to me. When they talk to you, they can all tell the same story

(Continued)

(Continued)

> [What I called earlier the ability "to talk the walk."] Every-
> one has this sense of gameplay. There is this system drive
> where people are conscious of making sure that they work
> together to improve the quality for everyone.

There is much more that could be said about the Queensland
strategy, such as how leaders are selected and trained and how the
senior ones (the deputy director and the seven regional directors)
develop as a team, but we have seen the essence of a strategy that
turned around the culture of a large, sprawling entity that went from
silos to synergy in four years. And it appears to be working, according to Watterston:

> After so many years of being ranked the seventh state or
> territory, results are really starting to kick in, [with respect
> to student results in] years three and five, for example. You
> know that people want to argue who's the fastest moving,
> but certainly the results in Queensland have been amazing.

I can also attest that John Hattie's impact analysis on basic results
now shows Queensland as the state with the most progress year over
year compared to the other states and territories. I asked Watterston if
there was one last point that he might want to make about the nature
of system success. He talked about the need to be out in the system
constantly learning and messaging. Top leaders can be out there messaging, but this can work only if they have something concrete and
insightful to say; they can get the latter only by trusting and interacting. In this process they get informed and become influential because
they have built trusted relationships and because they have something tangible to offer. Watterston concludes by saying that leaders
can try to play it safe by keeping their distance and hoping for limited
stress. Or they can be front and center telling the story that they learn
through their closeness to the field.

I think as a leader, what I've learned or had reinforced more and more is that people expect me to succinctly and enthusiastically tell the story: what are we up to, how are we doing this, and how do you think we are going? The story is not about what the director general is doing. I have to keep linking the story up. They want to know that the leaders know what they are doing.

Yes, trusting and interacting put the leader in a position to link the story up. Watterston also notes that rarely does it work to tell people what to do. He concludes:

You have to make sure that people are absolutely informed, that you demonstrate what good practice looks like, and that standards are set. You have to be seen to be fair. I think that for a really big organization, I have to be prominent. I have to know what's going on. I have to talk to people. I have to make sure that people see themselves as change agents in the organization.

There is a lot of nuance in what Jim Watterston and his colleagues do. But when you open it up as I did through the interviews, it becomes accessible. Indeed, it becomes more accessible to the very leaders themselves—who were not aware of some of their own nuances. There are a reasonably small number of key principles required, but they must be learned through deliberate practice that can be transparently and clearly stated. Talking the walk, and walking the talk, is a two-way street. In terms of nuance, recall Jody Gittell, who studied performance in the airline and hospital industries. It was the close reciprocal relations between leaders and those doing front line work that made the difference in which "managers learn from workers' deeper more focused knowledge of the work, and workers learn from managers' broader contextual knowledge" (p. 51).

(Continued)

(Continued)

Gittell gives a nod to Mary Parker Follett in describing this type of leadership as "coordinating of all functions, that is, a collective self-control" (p. 51). This is our culture-based accountability in action.

Finally, I should stress that nuanced leaders are system thinkers who pay attention to detail as they think about the big picture. Gittell (2016) captures this:

> The principles of shared goals, shared knowledge, and mutual respect are relevant at many levels, including (1) relationships between individuals; (2) relationships between groups; (3) relationships between organizations; and (4) relationships between regions . . . (p. 272). And, relational coordination is about the little things that add up to make a big difference. (p. 266)

Gittell identifies the bottom line of how systems change: "Changing structures and policies requires first enacting and living the changes in a way that helps others to visualize the change that is needed and to see why it is both possible and desirable to create this change" (Gittell, 2016, p. 266).

Case Example Ten
Integrating Accountability and Improvement
Whittier Union High School District, California

Our team has been working intensively in California for the past six years. We have been involved with some school districts that were successful under conditions of imposed top-down accountability (e.g., the decade 2000–2010), and others in recent times when the central policy has been more supportive and less imposed. I decided to take an example from the former time period, i.e., when state policy was characterized by top-down accountability. In this instance,

I examine a case study we conducted of Whittier Union High School District just east of Los Angeles (Fullan, 2016).

Whittier Union High School District consists of five comprehensive high schools, one continuation school, one alternative studies program, and one adult school. It serves about 13,000 students, of whom 83% are Hispanic and 80% socioeconomically disadvantaged. Student performance in WUHSD has improved in a sustained manner for over 15 years, with a higher portion of students graduating on time. It is a district that has consistently outperformed its counterparts year after year. Whittier superintendent Sandy Thorstenson, who retired in 2016, developed a small central team whose main strategy was to focus on teacher collaboration within and across schools. One main strategy consisted of establishing teacher-led course-by-course committees chaired by teachers with administrators serving as members on each committee. Common assessments were developed and linked to good pedagogy that was shared through networks of teachers. Groups of teachers design common assessments in teams for each subject according to state standards. The whole district is an exemplar of what I called earlier "precision over prescription." On a regular basis, assessments are linked to instructional strategies and in turn to evidence of impact on student learning, which then serves as input for the next round of teacher-led meetings.

Principals also play a key role within schools. They keep in constant communication with department chairs and are regular participants in teacher-led meetings. All high school principals meet as a group each Monday with the superintendent and other district leaders. Progress is regularly reviewed in order to identify what additional support or intervention may be needed. In our interviews with teachers and administrators, they identified teacher leadership, transparent communication, and trust as the basis of their success. They might as well have said "trust and interact." When you have a focused learning culture, by definition feedback is built in—what we call "learning is the work." Teachers who don't thrive under these conditions are more likely to leave voluntarily. Overall the system is so effective

(*Continued*)

(Continued)

that there is less need for formal evaluation of teachers. The system operates in a way that builds an ongoing pool of talent for leadership positions. We calculated that two in every five teachers in the district were participating in leadership groups in 2015, thereby providing daily leadership as well as establishing a strong pool of future school and district leaders. When Sandy retired, she was replaced by Martin Plourde, a senior member of the executive group. There has also been some turnover of principals and assistant principals over the past two years with no apparent change in the Whittier culture, as positive equitable results for students continue to accrue.

In some ways, the Whittier case is not an example of nuanced leadership, as it seems like good common practice. But when we think of the number of districts that have similar sounding visions but show limited results, you begin to appreciate that the "devil is in the details," to borrow a phrase from the parallel book we are writing (Gallagher & Fullan, forthcoming). Whittier's success under conditions of strong state accountability calls to mind another of our sticky phrases: "You may be stuck with state policy, but you are not stuck with the state mindset." Accountability—inside the culture of the organization—can be effective under a variety of external conditions.

> You may be stuck with state policy, but you are not stuck with the state mindset.

CULTURE COUNTS

Culture-based accountability includes external intervention. It's just that it is used selectively, i.e., when persistent failure occurs or in cases of fiscal or other malfeasance. Formal evaluation and intervention is *not* the norm in successful organizations. Most of the function of evaluation is covered by the specific interactive culture. To test this, partially at least, when Joanne Quinn and I wrote the book *Coherence,* we selected a small sample of school people we knew who were successful as leaders and asked them a straightforward question: Define accountability for us. They did not know on what basis they were selected. Here are three responses we got:

> Accountability is now primarily described as an accountability for learning. It is less about some test result and more about accepting ownership of the moral imperative of having every student learn. Teachers talk differently about "monitoring." As they engage in greater sharing of their work, they talk about being accountable to the school community looking to see what is changing for students as a result. (Fullan & Quinn, 2016, pp. 116–117)

More succinctly:

> When you blow down the doors and walls, you can't help but be ever more accountable. (pp. 116–117)

And,

> Teachers and administrators talk about accountability by de-privatizing their practices. If everyone knows what the other teacher is working on, and how they are working on it with students, it becomes easier to talk about accountability. (pp. 116–117)

It is neither natural nor effective to motivate humans through surveillance. Nuance leaders find more indirect means of carrying the day. They do so through purposeful interaction, which generates specific on-the-spot ongoing feedback. The tools of accountability are not instruments to be wielded, but cultures to be built. Even in the heavy-handed case of Benjamin Adlard where the state declared the school inadequate, local leaders had a choice about how to handle the situation. Marie-Claire Bretherton chose the nuanced way—below the surface, carefully nurturing and developing humanity, a relentless focus on the ball (improved teaching linked to results), collective efficacy, and identity.

I am struck by the two faces of accountability that Tim Brighouse and Viviane Robinson identified. Brighouse lamented the "thunderbolts of disruption" that came in the form of national prescriptions. Robinson was concerned about weak processes of interaction unlinked to outcomes that characterize the history of the teaching profession. What is remarkable is that they both recommend the *same solution*—improve the inside! At the end of the day improvement and accountability for the nuanced leader are one and the same. They are both culture-based.

Earlier in this chapter I said that I would return to the matter of so-called bad variation, which in reality is ineffective teaching. In culture-based accountability, bad variation gets taken care of naturally as teachers interact and sort out what is working or not. Weak practices get jettisoned and better ones get retained without great fanfare. At the same time good variation—innovations with promise—get tested and refined. The principal as lead learner does not have to judge these phenomena as an outsider because he or she is there, participating as a learner. Culture-based accountability uses the power of lateral learning, but it is focused and specific, not diffuse.

Don't get me wrong. We still need external assessment that has consequences for low performing schools and for high performing schools for that matter (they should be recognized and learned from). But internal or culture-based accountability is more important to develop because that is what exists at the end of each day. We saw this clearly in the cases of Marie-Claire Bretherton and Dr. Durán. In short, develop external systems of accountability while at the same time cultivate internal accountability in schools and sets of schools. The two systems—external and internal—work best when there is two-way interaction between them.

The bottom line is that if you can't account for yourself, you are not being accountable. The extra complication in education or any other human endeavor is that you are part of a group that must be accountable. We have seen that group accountability is quite a sophisticated challenge. These days there is an extra and compelling reason for ramping up our collective responsibilities. To put it bluntly as I did earlier, climate, economic, social, racial, and class problems are sweeping the world. New, more serious forms of accountability will be required: ones that are built into the culture of organizations. If any societal institution has a chance of changing our course, it has to be education. It is crunch time, and that is the subject of Chapter 5.

5

nuanced leaders
and the world

One thing about the immediate future that I know for a certainty is that inequality will continue to worsen in most societies to the point of straining social cohesion to the limit and perhaps destroying it altogether. This is because the forces causing it are so powerfully embedded and have enormous combinatory momentum. As humans we are in trouble. In this closing chapter I revisit the big picture, position education in its proper role of serving *all students*—a move that can be done only by "attacking inequity" with everyone in mind—and I re-examine the role of nuanced leaders as saviors in the equation.

MORE MACRO

In Chapter 1, I made the case that humanity is headed to a future fraught with unknowns, complexities, and catastrophic danger signs, and that we can no longer depend on our natural evolutionary forces to save the day. Recall Brooks, Damasio, Ford, Ramo, McAfee & Brynjolfsson, and others. These futurists (more accurately presentists) served up an array of bad knowns, bad unknowns, and mysterious combinations that look as if they will not end well. Now I want to add a couple of more trends that are hidden and pernicious and that we would not have uncovered without the instincts of nuanced investigators. The first concerns the automated health care system in the United States, and the second involves what the author refers to as "artificial (un)intelligence." I will also throw in the "money system." Once uncovered, all three represent a creeping and creepy feeling that our "systems" are beyond us—a kind of negative singularity is upon us.

Political science professor Virginia Eubanks (2017) conducted an exhaustive examination in two cities of how the growing automated "social services" systems were affecting the poor. One case focused on housing resources in Los Angeles, and the other on a child welfare agency in Pittsburgh. I will leave the reader to read the heart-rending cases of what amounts to the destruction of already poor people, but here is Eubanks's central finding:

> What I found was stunning. Across the country, poor and working class people are targeted by new tools of digital poverty management and face life-threatening consequences as a result. Automated eligibility systems discourage them from claiming public resources that they need to survive and thrive . . . Predictive models and algorithms tag them as risky investments and problematic parents. Vast complexes of social service, law enforcement, and neighborhood surveillance make their every move more visible and offer up their behavior for government, commercial, and public scrutiny. (p. 11)

Eubanks leaves little doubt about the effect of these systems that cast more and more people (not just the desperately poor) in digital poorhouses:

"automated decision-making shatters the social safety net, criminalizes the poor, intensifies discrimination, and compromises our deepest human values" (p. 12). In the end, concludes Eubanks, "automated tools for classifying the poor, left on their own, will produce towering inequalities" (p. 200).

Systemic discrimination would be the word—a system that no one designed intentionally but in a careless society is inevitable as technology marches on. The growing field of artificial intelligence raises similar issues. Insider software developer Meredith Broussard (2018), referring to "artificial unintelligence," draws the same conclusion about computers more generally as Eubanks did about digitally categorizing the poor:

> When we look at the world through the lens of computation, or we try to solve big social problems using technology alone, we tend to make a set of the same predictable mistakes that impede progress and reinforce inequality. (p. 7)

Even more telling:

> Being good with computers is not the same as being good with people. We shouldn't rush to be governed by computational systems designed by people who don't care about or don't understand the cultural systems in which we are all embedded. (p. 83)

Broussard's main point is that if we just leave it to machines and those who program them, we will end up with bad or misleading data. She concludes: "humans plus machines outperform humans alone or machines alone" (p. 175). But like Eubanks, Broussard finds that machines have gained the upper hand as human presence gets lost in the translation. In her words, "we need to add nuance to the way we talk about all things digital" (p. 87). Broussard too knows about the critical need to look below the surface to see what is really going on.

I could add more detail about what has happened and is happening in the money system. It is the same story, and if you want to immerse yourself in the particulars, read Jane Mayer's (2016) 500-page investigative account of what "dark money" has been to up to over the last 50 years—the growing concentration of money possessed by the less than 1% of the population in the United States (and trending similarly in more and more countries), resulting in a world of profound and ever widening economic inequality.

All of this adds up to one giant step for technology and one enormous blow to humanity—the cementing of extreme inequality. Aside from the dangers of denouement for all of us, it ain't good for those at the top either. Wilkinson and Pickett (2019) found that the richest 10% of people in high-inequality countries were more socially anxious than the bottom 10% in low-inequality countries. Stated differently, the more unequal the society, the more anxious that *everyone* becomes! We no longer have a segmented social justice issue; we have a system problem.

> Education has lost ground over the past 40 years as it sinks with other institutions toward locked-in inequality.

We should all be concerned about these developments and take action as citizens of today preparing for tomorrow. There is much policy and political work to be done. But I am addressing a more particular place. Education, long thought to be an instrument of democracy, enlightenment, and prosperity, has an urgent and critical role to play, starting immediately. Education has lost ground over the past 40 years as it sinks with other institutions toward locked-in inequality. My colleagues and I believe that education can reclaim this role as individual and societal savior, that the means of doing so are becoming clearer, and that vast majorities of the public want this to be done (although many will believe it only when they see it).

We do need a concentration of work at the education policy level of the kind being conducted by Linda Darling-Hammond and the Learning Policy Institute at Stanford. But my focus in this book is on leadership at the local and intermediate level where the development and mobilization of nuanced leaders has a strong chance of changing the system. The remaining two sections address the possibilities, first, within the education system itself, and second, through the expansion of nuance leaders in the mix.

LEARNERS AND CHANGE AGENTS:
ATTACK INEQUITY AND THRIVE ON EVERY LEVEL

We have already seen some of the ingredients of this solution in the 10 case study vignettes from our nuanced leaders. We can start with the same problems we see on a widespread basis: increased inequality, greater anxiety and stress among all groups of students, boredom or alienation relative to conventional schooling, realization that even getting good grades up to and including high school graduation does not prepare students for postsecondary education or for life itself. The good news is that we now see some light at the end of the tunnel.

The barriers are still formidable. I like how Linda Nathan, the founding head of the Boston Arts Academy (BAA), portrays the challenges facing her school in her book *When Grit Isn't Enough* (2017). The book shows how her school should have been a winner for the disadvantaged students that populated the school. It examines "how poverty and inequality thwart the college-for-all promise" even when conditions at the school level are seemingly favorable. In Nathan's firsthand account we discover how the hidden and not-so-hidden systemic barriers pertaining to money and race take their toll on many of the students, but we also see the promise—a promise that I will build on later in this section. Even with apparent counseling and financial support, Nathan describes how unpredictable financial costs took their toll on student motivation and ability to stay the course. While guaranteed some basic tuition, poor students found themselves confronted with hidden costs or missed deadlines that led to inability to continue. While race was less an issue at BAA where most students were from minority groups and supports were built in, graduating students had different experiences once they got to college. Some direct racism was encountered, but most of all, what took its toll was being left on your own as an individual where there was no social support and where being a minority student was too difficult for individuals to navigate through an impersonal bureaucracy.

What Nathan rails against is the assumption that the individual—in this case a minority student—will figure it out:

> What all the talk about grit seems to miss is the importance of putting children's experience front and center. In other words, when

the emphasis on grit ends up as a stand-alone pedagogy, the context of students' life and family circumstances is ignored. (p. 76)

Single-factor solutions—in this case, grit as a stand-alone solution—have no nuance. Nuance involves the *interaction and its effects* of a few critical factors—the latter being the constellation of specifics that surrounds the student's life. Giving out rewards for being "gritty," as some charter schools do, seems about as far from true learning as you can get.

In the examples of eventually successful students at BAA, we begin to see possible pathways to success for all, but especially for disadvantaged students (and in fact this is where we are going to end up in this section). Nathan describes it this way:

> Imagine a curriculum that is structured in such a way as to strengthen students' sense of self and their sense of inclusion in a supportive community. This can help young people develop a positive sense of agency and belonging—both important conditions for beneficial personal and collective development. (p. 142)

I maintained earlier that conventional schooling, including the almost sole emphasis on literacy and numeracy and high school graduation as ends in themselves, reinforced by high-stakes tests, has boxed in students and their schools, leading to a life of boring learning. Don't get me wrong. Literacy, numeracy, and high school graduation are necessary, but no longer sufficient; and the way they are being currently pursued is counterproductive for the deeper learning that is required for surviving, let alone thriving in 2020 and beyond. Today's schooling has a greater impact on the already disconnected, but also adversely affects the vast majority of students. Nathan identifies this very problem: "It is frustrating to know that the kind of learning involved to pass standardized tests does not bolster students' sense of agency or belonging, and there is little room for the learning that would" (p. 158).

To repeat, literacy and other basics are critical but become limited if they are a stand-alone focus. Shortly, I will make the case that deep learning does represent agency and belonging, as it increases literacy and numeracy even better than traditional means. Nathan picks up the story of a student named June, one of the successful alums of BAA who engaged in a project to study what other schools were doing (charters and district schools). June reports:

> We were interested in whether students had a sense of their own agency in their schools. Did they feel that schools were connected to their lives. (p. 159)

Now a teacher, June concludes: "it is urgent for traditional schools to think more broadly about what they want [to] accomplish with young people; the way they are doing it now isn't working" (p. 159).

Seeing many of her well-supported students experience success while at the school only to fail at university also caused Nathan to rethink the role of schooling:

> I now consider the most important purposes for schooling to be:
>
> - Helping students understand the context of their lives
> - Empowering students to create social change and solve problems that will improve living conditions and increase well-being
> - Teaching students to embrace differences and get along with others
> - Providing skill development, as well as opportunities for joy, beauty, play, and playfulness (p. 165)

Nathan's conclusions are remarkably similar to our own current work on deep learning, which I presented as Case Example Two (Ottawa), and Case Example Eight (deep learning globally). Deep learning is learning that sticks with you the rest of your life. It focuses on the 6Cs as learning goals and outcomes: character, citizenship, collaboration, communication, creativity, and critical thinking. It immerses students, usually in small teams, in selecting and working on problems that have personal meaning, purpose, and benefit for themselves and the world. It fundamentally alters the pedagogy of learning where students, teachers, and others operate as co-equal learning partners. Most of all, students get a taste of what it is like to be an agent of change and become committed to making a difference in the world locally and otherwise. Crucially, we have growing proof that deep learning, well done, produces scores of students as change agents already immersed in improving society at home and abroad (Fullan, Quinn, & McEachen, 2018).

The amazing thing is that we did not set out to produce these particular outcomes. We just wanted to make learning more interesting. Being creative, finding one's niche, fulfilling oneself, helping humanity, rectifying wrongs, worrying and doing something about the future all become part of the natural curriculum—*because deep learning appeals to the natural instincts of young people who are bored inside the walls of schools while the world outside churns.*

> Deep learning appeals to the natural instincts of young people who are bored inside the walls of schools while the world outside churns.

This is not some kind of whipped-up idealism, but rather speaks to the instincts of young people in today's world. There are few things worse than finishing school at any level and not knowing who you are. It also speaks profoundly to inequality and serves as an opening for schooling to serve as an agent of change in a way that it has never been able to take up.

I want to be careful here about where we are going with this. The strictures of inequality related to racism, poverty, gender, and sexual preference are deeply rooted and may not be movable. But for the first time in 50 years education has an opening, even a pathway. Attacking inequity with deep learning is the way forward. Deep learning—the 6Cs (or something like it) and related pedagogy—is good for all students but especially good for those least connected to conventional schooling.

Here is the hypothesis. By opening up the 6Cs, especially character, citizenship, and creativity, we activate, uncover or cause many students' natural propensity for doing something interesting and of value for themselves and for others. You literally "light up" students who appeared lifeless about learning, who in turn link with other students in a process that can only be called "positive contagion." By making disconnected students a priority in relation to meaningful, personal learning with others, you reach another tranche of non-learners.

For example, one school in Australia that we work with uses a phenomenon called "canary children" to reach otherwise neglected children, (see box on facing page).

I have used the "canary child" stimulus in my own workshops, and invariably 90% of the group can readily think of one or more such children in their own classrooms or schools. They are then stimulated to think of what they could have done differently to try to reach such a child.

Canary Child: A Catalyst for Deep Learning

Adapted from Rebecca Wells, 2018

The term *canary down the mine* has been used in many contexts, but no term better describes the warning signals given to teachers by students as they disengage from learning. Just as the canary was a good indicator of imminent danger to the miner, our canary children are sending constant warnings about the state of education in our classrooms, schools and systems. The difference is, however, that where workers in mines were taught to look for distress signals in their birds, teachers are taught no such thing. When a student is not behaviourally or cognitively engaged in the learning, the problem is thought to lie with the student, rather than the environment, content or mechanisms of the teaching. There are myriad reasons given for this, from learning disabilities, poverty or disadvantaged home situations, to laziness and poor attitude. In short, the child is scrutinised for not fitting the pedagogy, rather than the other way round.

Canaries and students, it turns out, are not too dissimilar in how they show their distress. Canaries ruffle their feathers, hide their heads beneath their wings and jump to other perches in their cage to try and escape unfavourable conditions. How many students, unable to follow the learning, falling behind, disinterested and disempowered, will also ruffle their feathers and create a scene, or hide away quietly, hoping not to be noticed?

Every classroom has at least one canary child, if not several. They are the students whose sense of purpose and self-esteem is slowly eroded through exposure to systems they are not compatible with, or learning they are not connected to. They are the children who don't fit, don't belong, can't keep up or can't see any meaningful purpose in the tasks and work they are asked to do. They are victims of their environment and a system that increasingly values competition over personal best, a system that strives to churn out ever higher scores to compete on local and global rankings,

(Continued)

(Continued)

rather than striving to produce productive, empowered and creative citizens.

These students eventually become the youth who disengage. They leave our schooling systems in increasing numbers worldwide, at great personal cost to their own futures, and diminishing the potential talent pool and contribution to the well-being of the entire human race. This same group remain marginalised beyond age 19, undereducated and underemployed. The proportion of canary children is at least 25%, and much more if we include all children who are not engaged in learning.

However, rather than cause for concern, the canary child should be viewed as a gift. They offer teachers, schools, districts and policy makers an opportunity to reset the direction of education, and rewrite the journey. They demand discussion and debate about who exactly education is for, simply by showing that it isn't working for them. They are the proof that things must change so that the educational experience is relevant, meaningful, authentic and purposeful. They are the catalyst to awaken us to the realisation that success must be attainable for every single child, and that learning be intentionally designed, systemwide, to engage, challenge, excite and provide the conditions for all children to thrive.

Underground, miners watched their birds diligently. They were acutely aware that any discomfort or signs of distress in their birds could result in their own deaths. There was an urgency to their relationship. For teachers, schools and systems, there is no real threat to their existence if a student falls through the cracks. In many cases there is even a benefit to the disengagement from schooling from underperforming students. One less underachieving student increases overall scores in measures that rank students, schools, systems and even countries, from high school certificates and tertiary entry rankings in secondary schools to global PISA rankings.

As long as we sustain education systems that value the end result over the journey, we fail our children. When we fail our children, we fail our society. We fail as human beings. Yet there is plenty of

> reason for hope. Right across the world deep learning is "attacking inequity" by engaging canary children. Still it is not enough. We need to make this a social movement of grand proportions.

It is not going to be easy, as we see from Carla Shalaby's (2017) up-close ethnographic account of four "canary children" that she studied that were deeply alienated from the group. My point in any case is that by making this quest explicit (attack inequity with deep learning), and by altering learning in a way that we know works with students, we could reach many more students than we do now.

We saw in the case of Dr. Durán in Chapter 3 that courageous, nuanced leaders can "shatter inequity" through deliberate, persistent, adaptable means. If 65% of high school students are not engaged now (as the data show), what if we reduced that percentage to 20%? We have some reason to believe that, with a focused effort, this may not take as long as we might think. Students are natural change agents, and once working on worthwhile developments, they move at the speed of social movements. And, remember, it is not just traditionally disconnected kids who are alienated and uninvolved, but also scores of others from backgrounds that used to enjoy or at least do well in schools. Use the group to change the group, and all will benefit.

In sum, in this book we have seen the desperate need at the individual and societal levels for major change; we have strong signals about the strategies and pathways that will be required to radically change course; we have seen that such changes on scale may well benefit all. I must say that the goal has to be to achieve equity of *outcome* (which means that no subgroup will perform on average at a level below any other subgroup). In the meantime, what has happened is that social mobility has become a scarce *individual* phenomenon. Compared to the 1970s, today only a few individuals move up with little overall social benefit. It is time to put the *social* back into social mobility and enable whole groups of the underserved to move up through greater education and corresponding well-being. The outcome we should be seeking should be at a much higher level than the present, entailing the development of the global competencies—the 6Cs or similar goals. I believe that this goal of equity outcomes at a higher level is achievable and, without a hint of exaggeration, essential for the survival of humankind. We need nuanced leaders in this quest because they know that anything less than what I propose is tinkering while the world burns.

BEING AND BECOMING A NUANCED LEADER

Let's start by returning to our definition of nuanced leadership that was set out in Chapter 1:

> **Nuance leaders** have a curiosity about what is possible, openness to other people, sensitivity to context, and a loyalty to a better future. They see below the surface, enabling them to detect patterns and their consequences for the system. They connect people to their own and each other's humanity. They don't lead; they teach. They change people's emotions, not just their minds. They have an instinct for orchestration. They foster sinews of success. They are humble in the face of challenges, determined for the group to be successful, and proud to celebrate success. They end up developing incredibly accountable organizations because the accountability gets built into the culture. Above all, they are courageously and relentlessly committed to changing the system for the betterment of humanity.

This, of course, is more of a gestalt than a checklist. Then I infused the definition with three traits that seemed to capture the work of what I would call "nuanced leaders in action." These were joint determination, adaptability, and culture-based accountability. Here lies the danger. This is not a playbook of three discrete tactics. It is more of a synergy of fused action. My colleague and leadership consultant (in sports, business, and education) Brendan Spillane from Australia immediately grasped the problem when he read a first draft of the manuscript:

> I wondered if it would take an already "nuanced" sensibility to get what you are saying. The already "nuanced leader" will see the JAC model as almost the underlying grammar of nuance, open to exception, stressed in the moment differently, open to being ignored if meaning/efficacy is enhanced by other means. They

will understand the need for orchestration for the power of the change music to be heard. The unnuanced leader will see it as a recipe; three discrete things to do, something to have workshops on and to develop leadership "capacity" via programs. They may see the three components as sections of an orchestra (wood, percussion, etc.) with each requiring practice. (personal communication, June 8, 2018)

Start worrying now because Spillane is probably right. Nuance leaders these days realize that they are in a particular moment of history when transformation is required from an unworkable present to an unknown future. It is this deep philosophy related to the fight of a lifetime that must characterize the transformation that I am talking about in this book. While we are getting advice from a sports consultant, let's delve into a relevant example. James Kerr's (2013) wonderful book, *Legacy: What the All Blacks Can Teach Us About the Business of Life*, on the perennial success of New Zealand's All Blacks rugby team, is instructive for our purpose.

The All Blacks' first stance is about "Challenge," which refers to facing formidable opposition that must be defeated and is accompanied by the idea of how little time is given to us, and "this is our time" (Kerr, 2013, p. viii). For the All Blacks, the opposition is the opposing team; for us, try "deep inequity" as the foe. Nuanced leaders know that this is the fight of a lifetime. Consider the other themes in the All Blacks' makeup: character, adaptability, purpose, responsibility, learning ability, Whanau (a Maori term referring to extended family, and often described as "flying in the same direction"), preparation, pressure, authenticity, sacrifice, language, ritual, Whakapapa (interdependence of our past, present, and future), and legacy. Talk about mirroring a deep nuanced culture! The unified group is in the fight of a lifetime; the enemy is powerful; you must win this one. It is your job to be a good ancestor today for tomorrow. It is *that* serious. The message then is to be nuanced about nuance. Work on what underlies the three traits of nuance (joint determination, adaptability, and culture-based accountability) and identify, and their unification. To do this we need to continue to explore the underlying premise of nuance and get better at it.

One further key point. Nuance leaders are especially attuned to *context*. They know that each context is different and are especially sensitive to its particulars. This is a crucial insight. The three nuance traits that I identified are themselves abstractions from context. The case study interviewees in this book were not just talking about joint determination, adaptive alterations, and culture-based accountability in general, but rather their particular manifestations *in the settings in which they work.* This means that if you are going to use the ideas in this book effectively, you will need to spend time understanding the specifics of the group you are leading in that culture: its history, values, tensions, power distributions, hidden frustrations, and desires. Empathy for context is an essential requirement for making change with the people who live the context every day. When it comes to given situations, there are no shortcuts to nuance.

> Empathy for context is an essential requirement for making change with the people who live the context every day.

Over 50 years ago, Michael Polanyi in *The Tacit Dimension* said, "we can know more than we can tell" (1966, p. x). I take this to mean that through purposeful action we can uncover and build on what we subconsciously might know. Polanyi also offers the following tease: "an unbridled lucidity can destroy our understanding of complex matters" (p. 18). Absence of nuance (surface knowledge) is worse than we thought: it can give us a false sense of clarity—thinking we know something that we don't know. Unbridled lucidity is false precision.

How do we go about combating undetected falsehoods? Amazingly (I think), Michael Polanyi and Leonardo da Vinci agree on the answer. First Polanyi: "It is not by looking at things, but by *dwelling in them,* that we understand their joint meaning" (1966, p. 18, my italics).

Joint can refer to surface or deep meaning. Recall Isaacson's capturing of Leonardo's method of learning, which was that getting at the *experience* of others was a means of understanding them. Leonardo was "a disciple of experience and experiment"; he understood things and people because "my subjects require experience rather than the words of others" (p. 17); and, "my intention is to consult experience first and *then* with reasoning show why such experience is bound to operate in such a way" (p. 18, my italics added). Start with practice, journey to theory.

By the way, Leonardo's main problem, according to Isaacson, was that he was often "more easily distracted by the future than he was focused on the present" (p. 82). Nobody's perfect. Actually, Leonardo's modus operandi was quite complicated, not least because our knowledge of why he did what he did is flimsy. In a wonderfully irreverent book titled *Becoming Leonardo: An Exploded View of the Life of Leonardo da Vinci,* Mike Lankford (2017) takes liberties with gaps in history to fashion what could only be called a romp through the 67 years of Leonardo's life. Lankford uses a combination of facts, inferences, and other fragments to trace and construct Leonardo's thinking, actions, and life. Lankford infers that "Leonardo learned to *see* by looking ever more closely at those things around him" (p. 11). Or, "[He] seemed a man willing to wait for inspiration and insight. He seemed willing to study a thing until it spoke to him and revealed its secrets" (p. 22). One might say that nuance resides in the interaction of the genius of Leonardo as observer and the magnificence of what is being studied.

It is the case that Leonardo took a long time to complete things and was often torn between what he was contracted to do (when he needed money), and what he wanted to do which was much more exploratory. Even when he was doing what he presumably wanted, he took a long time. As Lankford interprets it, many people "start off with a burst and then dribble away at the end" (p. 128). By contrast, Leonardo "learned to leave and come back, to look with different eyes, different moods, different times day of the day—all these things allowed him to see better and to better understand" (p. 128). Perhaps we see here a confirmation of our change saying, "go slow to go fast," and the folly of going too fast early and getting nowhere.

I mentioned earlier that Leonardo was obsessed with detail, thereby enabling him to get at the inner workings of things in order to extrapolate to the big picture: micro to macro. You can't get solidly to the latter without immersing yourself first in the former. In his final chapter, Isaacson generates a list of 20 factors under the heading "Learning From Leonardo." More than half of the list is pure nuance: Be curious, relentlessly curious; see knowledge for its own sake; retain a childlike sense of wonder; observe; start with details; see things unseen; go down rabbit holes; get distracted ("we have to be fearless about changing our minds based on new information"); respect facts; procrastinate; let the perfect be the enemy of the good; think visually; avoid silos; let your reach exceed your grasp; indulge fantasy; create for yourself not for patrons; collaborate;

make lists; take notes on paper; and be open to mystery (Isaacson, 2017, pp. 519–524).

Returning to Polanyi for a moment, he has the following rather curious passage:

> Take two points, (1) tacit knowing of a coherent entity relies on our knowing of the particulars of the entity for attending to it; and (2) if we switch our attention to the particulars, this function of the particulars is cancelled and we lose sight of the entity to which we had attended. (Polyani, 1966, p. 34)

What Polyani is saying is that the laws governing the particulars and those governing the entity are different and cannot by definition be reconciled. System nuance draws a different conclusion. The micro and macro can and must be reconciled. Leonardo and Mary Parker Follett show that seeing the details, the bigger picture, and their interconnection is crucial for comprehending and orchestrating system change. John Malloy and Jim Watterston, for example, demonstrate how successful leaders manage to do just that!

Leonardo knew the difference between degrees of nuance when he said, "There are three classes of people: those who see; those who see when they are shown, those who do not see" (quoted in Lankford, 2015). My goal in this book is to make this less a static classification and more a frame for development. For starters, nuance leaders don't wake up one day, and all of a sudden can "see." Through the cases and actions I have described across the chapters, we see how successful leaders become more attuned to both detail and patterns, being careful to respect context in every new situation. Over time such leaders become more nuanced, often without realizing it. They gradually discover, usually with the people in the situation, promising pathways to better and more satisfying solutions to what they want to accomplish.

> The first lesson, then, for upping your nuance game is to participate observantly in both the micro and macro worlds, all the while connecting them as you go.

The first lesson, then, for upping your nuance game is to participate observantly in both the micro and macro worlds, all the while connecting them as you go. Take the All Blacks' advice and consider it an all-in proposition where your detailed savvy derives from following and leading the action. You will learn things that are not in the recipe book that add to your bank of nuanced knowledge.

The second lesson comes from how "the science of expertise" is developed, and is aided by recent insights from the neuroscience of learning as applied to adults. The 10,000-hour rule popularized by Malcolm Gladwell makes the case that almost anyone can become an expert if he or she puts in the 10,000 hours to get that good. The original researchers, Ericsson and Pool (2016), say "not so fast; there is more to it than the sheer number of hours. The secret is 'purposeful, deliberate practice.'" An encouraging basis, according to Ericsson and Pool, is that "no one has found the upper limits of long-term memory" (p. 2). In other words, if we can find the best method for making learning "stick," we can go way beyond where we are now. For Ericsson and Pool, that best method is "purposeful practice," which has four characteristics:

1. Well-defined specific goals

2. Is focused

3. Involves feedback

4. Requires getting out of one's comfort zone (p. 15)

We have already seen the importance of specific feedback *while* you are doing something. If a student gets belated feedback on a performance test, say, a C grade, or a putative leader gets only general or no feedback while doing his or her work—"there has been no feedback during practice—no one . . . pointing out mistakes with the student seemingly clueless about whether there were errors" (p. 17). If this is the predominant mode over time—say, 10 years' experience as a leader—you learn a few things through trial and error, but soon you reach a limit—a law of diminishing returns. Nuance takes us beyond that limit to never-ending learning.

Getting out of one's comfort zone takes us to that part of brain research that most people are ignorant of or don't understand that *some degree of anxiety* is necessary for growth. As Ericsson and Pool state: "Regular training [as in practice-based feedback] leads to changes in the parts of the brain that are challenged by the training" (p. 45).

Linking this to the findings in the "culture-based accountability" chapter, we can say that punitive accountability generates negative anxiety that stunts cognitive and emotional growth, while transparent, supportive, specific feedback causes a degree of anxiety that has exactly the right blend of pressure and support that moves us forward (and once we experience the success of the new behavior, we are motivated to do more of it, and thus consolidate it as part of our new repertoire, so to speak).

Ericsson and Pool also confirm our point about how seasoned experts have come to master detail *and* the bigger picture. Research on master chess players reveals that they

> quickly examine strings of possible moves and countermoves in great detail, looking for the particular move that will offer the best chance of winning. In short, while the mental representation gives masters a view of the forest that novices lack, they also allow masters to zero in on the trees when necessary. (p. 58)

Ericsson and Pool's conclusion:

> The main thing that sets experts apart from the rest of us is that their years of practice have changed their neural circuitry in their brains to produce highly specialized mental representations, which in turn make possible the incredible memory, pattern recognition, problem solving, and other sorts of advanced ability needed to excel in their particular specialties. (p. 63)

Beyond this, fields of expertise generate a subset of skilled practitioners who also serve as teachers, coaches, and mentors that over time "have developed increasingly sophisticated sets of . . . techniques that make possible the field's steadily increasingly skill level" (p. 86). Put another way, would-be nuancers need mentorship and coaching, and in turn, must play that role as they themselves get more proficient.

One last warning from Ericsson and Pool: be careful when identifying so-called "experts" because "research has shown that the 'experts' in many fields don't perform reliably better than other, less highly regarded members of the profession" (p. 105). Think of this when hiring your next superintendent: résumés, interviews, letters of reference and the like are less reliable than judgment of peers and subordinates who have seen the leader in action. This is why if you have a culture of "learning is the work," then promoting from within is more predictable, although there are times when external hiring is necessary.

What makes hiring doubly difficult is that by definition it is hard to hire for nuance. The bottom line is that experience and credentialed expertise do not confirm nuance. This is why it is essential to go the extra mile to find out how a person leads on the job. Ericsson and Pool warn us that it is a mistake to focus only on *knowledge.* You need to know what a person can do and how conscious he or she is about how to go about the work. If not attended to, tacit knowledge doesn't surface that often. This is why I would venture to say that Marie-Claire Bretherton, John Malloy, and Jim Watterston came to know more about their own leadership *after* I interviewed them than before. I was able to probe and raise to a level of explicitness aspects of their own tacit knowledge that once made transparent would be available to them (and others). There is no reason why current nuanced leaders could not become more aware of what they do and, in turn, mentor others to be similarly engaged and reflective. There is also no reason why any leader could not commit to becoming more nuanced through their own actions and learning. Such knowledge and skills in action can be continually refined. It is not more knowledge or more experience per se that makes a difference but rather what a person has learned relative to reading and acting on in given situations. Effective leaders have a particular nuance. They are sensitive to human action and interpersonal relationships and recognize that changing human dynamics is the key to significant improvement. They are fiercely committed to creating a better future with the people they lead.

> Any leader can commit to becoming more nuanced through their own actions and learning . . . and in turn mentor others to be similarly engaged and reflective.

All of this means that leaders can change and can be helped to change. Furthermore, this change can be deeper and more lasting than we might have predicted. By getting inside both the big and small picture (lesson one), and by engaging in immersive purposeful practice with feedback from mentors (lesson two), you can develop nuance. Put in your hours of deliberate practice and gain in two ways: the direct knowledge that you will acquire and the hidden effect on your brain—you will learn subconsciously to see patterns more readily. You will become a smarter leader without fully understanding how it happened.

We can take the case of Marie-Claire Bretherton from Benjamin Adlard (Chapter 2) to illustrate how intensive this development can be. In the interview I asked her how as a young leader she came to have the commitment and skill to take on such a desperate situation. Here is her response:

> Over the last 10 years I would say that my skills as a leader have been developed primarily through a combination of great mentorship within a rich tapestry and variety of leadership experiences— no two years have felt the same. When I first became a school leader, I felt like I was underqualified . . . As a result, I actively sought out as much help as I could from those around me, both peer and other leaders nationally who I admired. I deliberately invited others to help shape my thinking and my leadership. . . . The peer-to-peer review and the ongoing professional learning provided great nourishment. So, when I was asked to become the Executive Headteacher at Benjamin Adlard, I went into it with two key values underpinning my strategy—(1) I won't be able to do this on my own and (2) there is good in everyone—like that quote from Rumi—"where there is ruin, there is hope for a treasure." (personal communication, June 2018)

I also asked Bretherton why she took the Benjamin Adlard job. Her response was more elaborate than I expected. She explained first that her mentor, Steve Munby (former head of England's National College for Leadership), urged her to take the position, challenging her that this was a chance to prove what could be done. Then she expanded on her thinking:

> On a practical level, I was fearful that I didn't have enough capacity . . . I had never worked in a school with the level of challenge or disadvantage that Benjamin Adlard faced. It was well beyond my comfort zone. I was also worried that I would lose credibility in the eyes of my peers if I struggled to make the school better quickly—I knew all eyes would be on me . . . I felt that the

professional risks for me were also quite significant—some colleagues had told me that it would be "professional suicide."

Steve [Munby] called my bluff—he said something like "if you really believe in social justice and you really understand the wider moral purpose of education, then this is the school you need to be in right now—this is where you are needed most—this is where you can prove it and make a difference." He challenged my thinking about my capacity and asked me to consider what I would need to change to make it possible.

He didn't completely convince me, so I agreed to go and visit the school and see what I thought. It was worse that I had imagined. It had no perimeter fence, so the pupils were freely leaving the site when they'd had enough. The playground was a wasteland of concrete. The pupils were pale; some looked malnourished and unhappy. The acting headteacher had no sense of hope that things could ever be any better—she had lost faith in the system. I asked the acting head to tell me about each of the children that were in a special class of eight called "the nurture class." Their stories included backgrounds of child prostitution, trafficking, domestic abuse, parental drug abuse and alcoholism, child brutality, child pornography, as well as a history of exclusions in school, poor behaviour and very low attainment academically. None of these children were older than nine years of age.

The thing that broke my heart was not just that bad things had happened to these children, but it was that the staff had no hope that they could make any difference or make things any better. The staff had no aspirations, no vision and no hope—and the odds were stacked up against them. At that moment, I knew that Steve was right—I had to take the job. And even if I failed, I would fail trying to do what I believed was morally right. (personal communication, June 2018)

There is no getting around it: turning around seemingly hopeless situations is a monumental undertaking. It requires a kind of All Blacks commitment and engagement. But it is doable. You begin to realize what it takes to transform even the most intractable situations; it changes your brain for the better, thereby requiring less conscious effort; it becomes second nature; it helps scores of others. It makes a lasting difference.

In Chapters 2, 3, and 4, I laid out in some detail with concrete examples the workings of each of the three main components of the JAC Model: joint determination, adaptability, and creating a culture of accountability. We need to underscore that they work in concert. First, if you ask the question in relation to joint determination—Who has the upper hand? The leader or the followers?—then the answer is that in the best processes it is impossible to tell. Mary Parker Follet (2017) observed that the effective "group process is the one that expresses individual differences, and integrates them" (p. 63). If growth is by integration, the strands are impossible to separate. With characteristic perspicacity, Parker Follet states, "control brings disastrous consequences whenever it outruns integration" (p. 191). The role of the leader in joint determination is to come to the table with good ideas while generating new authority through the intermingling and integration of ideas and forces. In joint determination the idea of bosses and followers dissolves into unity of purpose that is a never-ending process. Unity of purpose is never static. It is constantly in formation even though, at a given time in the process, it can be captured as a state of play.

Adaptability clearly interacts with joint determination. When Mark Edwards in Mooresville made a radical shift from digital driven to culture driven, it was because of what he and his followers were experiencing and learning. When you combine the principles of joint determination and adaptability, it is impossible (and unnecessary) to discern who was the first to have the idea to make the change. Maybe nuanced leaders like Mark notice it first, but it had to be there to be noticed. And if it was there, it was because some participants on the ground were ahead of Mark in recognizing the need for a change in emphasis. Like many breakthrough ideas, it can be impossible to pinpoint the day the tide turned. But we do know that there would not have been a shift in focus had Mark and others not been close to the action—learning from what was happening day after day.

Adaptability is necessary all the more because the environment is awash with radical changes and unpredictability. Eric Ries (2017) writes about his experience as an entrepreneur in developing and consulting with start-ups:

> I have come to realize that today's organizations—both established and emerging—are missing capabilities that are needed for every organization to thrive on the century ahead: the ability to experiment rapidly with new products and new business models, the ability to empower their most creative people, and the ability to engage again and again in an innovation process—and manage it with rigor and accountability—so that they can unlock new sources of growth and productivity. (p. 3)

We also find in Ries a precise definition of adaptability: "the pivot, *a change in strategy without a change in vision*" (p. 108, italics in original).

Third, we have culture-based accountability that also reinforces daily interaction in conjunction with joint determination and adaptability. All three processes serve to create a process of checks and balances. Trust and interaction help jettison weak ideas, as they infuse new ones that get sorted out by the process. The whole set of actions are organic and depend on leaders who are skilled in the three processes of the JAC model, provided that they heed Spillane's advice cited above: It is "the underlying grammar of nuance stressed in the moment of action" that is the key to learning what to do.

To sum up, the model is not a matter of three steps or elements. In the 10 case examples, I highlighted which of the three elements was best illustrated in the case being examined, but in reality, the three elements reinforce each other to form an integrated whole. The ultimate power of nuance is in the synergy of the three. They operate in the service of greater equity and excellence for the organization or system as a whole.

It is encouraging to find that the work on effective strategies for helping individuals change for the better reinforces the findings of nuance. A policy paper from the London policy entity Nesta examined the difference between "good and bad help." The researchers found that bad help skimmed the surface with "too many initiatives," "imposed solutions," "engaged in negative monitoring," and "neglected key factors that under-mined implementation." By contrast, good help worked on people's "sense of purpose," "confidence and capability to act," and supportive "life circumstances" relative to the change direction (Wilson et al., 2018). The message is clear for leaders: examine whether you are unwittingly a surfacer, or whether you are prepared to enter the world of nuance with definite strategies that will challenge you, but from which you will learn. The learning will be natural and continuous and will pull you forward into the depths of change that are so crucial to address as society grapples with complexity, opportunities, and dangers never before faced by humanity. The next period is crucial. Never before have nuanced leaders been more needed.

The good news is that nuance can be learned. All of the leaders we examined in this book got stronger and stronger over time through what they experienced and learned. They became stronger characters and more courageous as a result of what they learned. Formation comes hand-in-hand with action as nuance leaders go deeper and deeper consolidating their learnings and processing their doubts. To me, it is a bit magical. If you integrate the three key themes of nuance, you end up being a better leader without realizing how and when it happened.

I can't help but think that nuance is related to human evolution that so far indicates that the brain and associated human values have a bias, but not a guarantee for becoming better and better. These values are being tested by what the neuroscientist Antonio Dasmasio calls "the strange order of things" in the present that he claims is getting stranger and stranger. We should still believe in the corrective power of social evolution, but it may need some assistance. Maybe the formulation of help that I am expressing in this book may already reflect the very act of evolution inevitably kick-ing in. No matter. I believe that the insights of nuance that I have identified in this book are a vital part of the solution. I am buoyed by these dis-coveries because they come from the detail of practice. As I have argued throughout the book, breakthrough ideas exist below the surface inside the depth of unseen interactions and processes.

The particular set of solutions that this book focuses on concern edu-cation. It has been often debated whether education is an agent of change or of preservation. It is both, depending on the times. The trend since post–World War II is interesting to observe. The United States, for example, had decades of progress from 1948 to 1988—more high school and university graduates reduction of the achievement gap between subgroups, and economic growth that benefited the majority. We now know that this trend has been reversed. There has been a fast moving and growing gap between the very rich and all others that has been galloping forward since the late 1980s—a gap that shows every indication of continuing full speed ahead. Under these conditions, McAffee and Brynjolsson (2017) conclude that there can be no reliable playbook for what to do because "there is simply too much change and too much uncertainty at present" (p. 27). They argue that the best way forward is to "predict less, experiment more," a proposition that could have come straight from the mouth of Leonardo, and that represents a clarion call for nuanced development and guidance.

Education, radically transformed, is our best hope forward. I am heartened by the emerging findings in deep learning that students from a very young age may be the best change agents that we have ever seen. The more disconnected that these students have been, the better force for change they can be, *if* we can reclaim them. They know what the downside feels and looks like. They have a natural propensity to *engage the world change the world.* This is where and how significant learning most naturally occurs. This is where humanity and networks intersect. This is where nuance lives. This is where leaders must live and learn.

Nuance leadership means leadership that is less obvious but more certain in its outcomes because it taps into the inner workings of productive human interaction. If only Leonardo da Vinci could see us now as we approach the 500th anniversary of his death, May 2, 1519!

references

Ahtiainen, R. E. (2017). *Shades of change in Fullan and Hargreaves' models* (Doctoral dissertation). University of Helsinki.

Argyris, C. (1999). *On organizational learning* (2nd ed.). Oxford: Blackwell Business.

Australian Institute for Teaching and School Leadership-AISTL. (2018). *Leading for impact: Australian guidelines for school leadership development.* Melbourne, AU: Author.

Avelar LaSalle, R., & Johnson, R. (2019). *Shattering inequities.* Washington, DC: Rowman & Littlefield.

Boston Consulting Group. (2014). *Teachers know best: Teachers' views on professional development.* Washington, DC: Gates Foundation.

Bretherton, Marie-Claire. (2018). Interview with Michael Fullan, Birmingham, England, June 14, 2018.

Brooks, D. (2018). The strange failure of the educated elite. *The New York Times.* Retrieved from www.nytimes.com/2018/05/28/opinion/failure-educated-elite.html

Broussard, M. (2018). *Artificial intelligence: How computers misunderstand the world.* Cambridge, MA: MIT Press.

Bryant, A. (2013). Honeywell's David Cote on decisiveness as a two-edged sword. *The New York Times.* Retrieved from http://www.nytimes.com

Bryk, A., Gomez, L., Grunow, A., & Le Mahieu, P. (2015). *Learning to improve: How America's schools can get better at getting better.* Cambridge, MA: Harvard University Press.

Campbell, D., & Fullan, M. (forthcoming). *The governance core: A systems approach to local decision making.* Thousand Oaks, CA: Corwin.

Chandler, T. (2016). *How performance management is killing performance.* Oakland, CA: Berrett-Koehler.

Cartwright, N., & Hardie, J. (2012). *Evidence-based policy.* Oxford: Oxford University Press.

Catmull, H. (2014). *Creativity Inc.: Overcoming the unseen forces that stand in the way of true transformation.* New York, NY: Random House.

Damasio, A. (2018). *The strange order of things: Life, feeling, and the making of cultures.* New York, NY: Pantheon.

Dintersmith, T. (2018). *What school could be: Insights and inspiration from teachers across America.* Princeton, NJ: Princeton University Press.

Duggan, W. (2007). *Strategic intuition: The creative spark in human achievement.* New York, NY: Columbia University Press.

Edwards, M. (2014). *Every child, every day: A digital conversion model for student achievement.* Upper Saddle Creek, NJ: Pearson Education Inc.

Edwards, M. (2016). *Thank you for your leadership: The power of distributed leadership in a digital conversion model.* Upper Saddle Creek, NJ: Pearson Education Inc.

Elmore, R. (2004). *School reform from the inside out: Policy practice and performance.* Cambridge, MA: Harvard University Press.

Eubanks, V. (2017). *Automating inequality: How high-tech tools profile, police, and punish the poor.* New York: St Martin's Press.

Ericsson, A., & Pool, R. (2016). *Peak: Secrets from the new science of expertise.* New York, NY: Houghton Mifflin Harcourt.

Freire, P. (2000). *Pedagogy of the oppressed.* New York, NY: Bloomsbury.

Ford, M. (2015). *The rise of robots: Technology and the threat of a jobless future.* New York, NY: Basic Books.

Fullan, M. (2010). *All systems go: The change imperative for whole system reform.* Thousand Oaks, CA: Corwin.

Fullan, M. (2011). *Choosing the wrong drivers for whole system reform.* Seminar Series 204. Melbourne, AU: Centre for Strategic Education.

Fullan, M. (2013a). *Stratosphere: Integrating technology, pedagogy, and change.* Toronto, ON: Pearson Canada.

Fullan, M. (2013b). *Motion leadership in action: More skinny on becoming change savvy.* Thousand Oaks, CA: Corwin.

Fullan, M. (2014). *The principal: Three keys for maximizing impact.* San Francisco, CA: Jossey-Bass.

Fullan, M. (2016). *California's golden opportunity: Whittier Union School District.* Toronto, ON: Motion Leadership.

Fullan, M. (2018). *Surreal change: The real life of transforming public education.* New York, NY: Routledge.

Fullan, M., & Boyle, A. (2014). *Big city school reforms: Lessons from New York, Toronto, and London.* New York, NY: Teachers College Press.

Fullan, M., & Edwards, M. (2017). *The power of unstoppable momentum: Key drivers to revolutionize your district.* Bloomington, IN: Solution Tree Press.

Fullan, M., & Hargreaves, H. (2016). *Bringing the profession back in: A call to action.* Oxford, OH: Learning Forward.

Fullan, M., & Pinchot, M. (2018). The fast track to sustainable turnaround. *Educational Leadership, 75*(75), 48–54.

Fullan, M., & Quinn, J. (2016). *Coherence: The right drivers in action for schools, districts, and systems.* Thousand Oaks, CA: Corwin.

Fullan, M., Quinn, J., & Adam, E. *Taking action guide to building coherence in schools districts, and systems.* Thousand Oaks, CA: Corwin.

Fullan, M., Quinn, J., & McEachen, J. (2018). *Deep learning: Engage the world Change the world.* Thousand Oaks, CA: Corwin.

Gallagher, M. J., & Fullan, M. (forthcoming). *System change: The devil is in the details.* Thousand Oaks, CA: Corwin.

Gittell, J. (2016). *Transforming relationships for high performance: The power of relational coordination.* Stanford, CA: Stanford University Press.

Hargreaves, A., & O'Connor, M. T. (2018). *Collaborative professionalism.* Thousand Oaks, CA: Corwin.

Hargreaves, H., & Shirley, D. (2018). *Leading from the middle: Spreading learning, well-being and identity across Ontario.* Toronto, ON: CODE Consortium.

Harris, A., & Jones, M. (2018). The dark side of leadership and management. *School Leadership and Management, 38*(5), 475–477.

Heifetz, R., & Linsky, M. (2017). *Leadership on the line: Staying alive through the dangers of change.* Boston, MA: Harvard Business School Press.

Héon, F., Davis, A., Jones-Patulli, J., & Damart, S. (Eds.). (2017). *The essential Mary Parker Follett* (2nd ed.). Author.

Isaacson, W. (2017). *Leonardo da Vinci.* New York, NY: Simon & Schuster.

Kellerman, B. (2004). *Bad leadership: What it is, how it happens, why it matters.* Boston, MA: Harvard Business Review Press.

Kerr, J. (2013). *Legacy: What the All Blacks can teach us about the business of life.* London: Constable.

Khanna, P. (2016). *Connectography: Mapping the future of global civilization.* New York, NY: Random House.

Kirtman, L., & Fullan, M. (2016). *Leadership: Key competencies for whole-system change.* Bloomington, IN: Solution Tree Press.

Koretz, D. (2017). *The testing charade: Pretending to make schools better.* Chicago, IL: University of Chicago Press.

Lankford, M. (2017). *Becoming Leonardo: An exploded view of the life of Leonardo da Vinci.* London: Melville House

MacBeath, J., Dempster, N., Frost, D., Johnson, G., & Swaffield, S. (2018). *Strengthening the connections between leadership and learning.* London: Routledge.

Malloy, J. (2018). Interview with Michael Fullan, Toronto, Ontario, March 30, 2018.

Martin, R., & Osberg, S. (2015). *Getting beyond better: How social entrepreneurship works.* Boston, MA: Harvard Business School Press.

McAfee, A., & Brynjolfsson, E. (2018). *Machine, platform, crowd: Harnessing our digital future.* New York, NY: W.W. Norton.

Metha, J. (2013). *The allure of order.* New York: Oxford University Press.

Mayer, J. (2017). *Dark money: The hidden history of the billionaires behind the rise of the radical right.* New York: Anchor Books.

New Pedagogies for Deep Learning. (2018). www.npdl.global

Ontario Ministry of Education. (2017). *Specialist high skills majors.* Toronto, ON: Author.

Pfeffer, J., & Sutton R. (2006). *Hard facts, dangerous half-truths, and total nonsense.* Boston, MA: Harvard Business School Press.

Ottawa Catholic School Board. (2018). Personal communication with Tom D'Amico, Associate Director of Education.

Polyanyi, M. (1996). *The tacit dimension.* Chicago, IL: University of Chicago Press.

Ramo, J. R. (2016). *The seventh sense: Power, fortune, and survival in the age of networks.* New York, NY: Little Brown.

Ries, E. (2017). *The startup way: How modern companies use entrepreneurial management to transform culture and drive long-term growth.* New York, NY: Crown Business.

Robinson, K., with L. Aronica. (2018). *You, your child, and school: Navigate your way to the best education.* New York, NY: Penguin.

Robinson, V. (2018). *Reduce change to increase improvement.* Thousand Oaks, CA: Corwin.

Rummelt, R. (2011). *Good strategy, bad strategy: The difference and why it matters.* New York, NY: Crown Business.

Sachs, J. (2018). *Unsafe thinking: How to be nimble and bold when you need it the most.* New York: Da Capo Lifelong Books.

Santalises, S. (2018). *Keynote.* Carnegie Foundation Summit on Improvement in Education. San Francisco, April 4, 2018.

Shalaby, C. (2017). *Troublemakers: Lessons in freedom from young children at school.* New York: The New Press.

Sutton, R., & Rao, H. (2014). *Scaling up excellence: Getting to more without settling for less.* New York, NY: Crown Business.

The Learning Exchange. (2018). *Deep learning: System level implementation.* Video. Retrieved from https://thelearningexchange.ca/videos/deep-learning-system-level-implementation. Toronto: Author.

Toronto District School Board. (2016). *A vision for learning.* Toronto, ON: Author.

Toronto District School Board. (2017). *Learning centres.* Toronto, ON: Author.

Toronto District School Board. (2016-2019). *Integrated equity framework.* Toronto, ON: Author.

Watterston, J. (2017). Interview with Michael Fullan, Melbourne, Australia, April 4, 2017.

Wells, C., & Feun, L. (2013). Education change and professional learning communities: A study of two districts. *Journal of Educational Change, 14*(2), 233–257.

Wilkinson, R., & Pickett, K. (2019). *The inner level: How equal societies reduce stress, restore sanity, and improve everyone's well-being.* New York: Penguin Press.

Wilson, R., Cornwell, C., Flanagan, E., Nielsen, N., & Khan, H. (2018). *Good and bad help: How purpose and confidence transform lives.* London: Nesta.

Index

acknowledgments

When you write a book called *Nuance,* how in the world are you going to remember who helped? As I said in my autobiography, my life is *Surreal,* which means that much of what I experience is in the stratosphere where ideas and insights get absorbed in mysterious ways. Nonetheless, here goes.

Tim Brighouse, Viviane Robinson, Brendan Spillane, and Santiago Rincón-Gallardo contributed directly in helping me nail down the concept of *Nuance*. Three key interviews with nuance leaders of the world gave substance to the ideas. I thank Marie-Claire Bretherton, John Malloy, and Jim Watterston for allowing me to get inside their minds, and roam around.

My team keeps going gangbusters on system improvement, local and worldwide. My sincere thanks to Eleanor Adam, Doug Ashleigh, Pam Betts, Alan Boyle, Matt Cane, Jean Clinton, Claudia Cuttress, Max Drummy, Mary Jean Gallagher, Mag Gardner, Peter Hill and Carmel Crévola, Bill Hogarth, Joanne McEachen, Charles Pascal, Joanne Quinn, Santiago Rincón-Gallardo, and Catie Shuster. Other practitioners helped: Robin Avelar La Salle, Miguel Brechner, Davis Campbell, Génie Congi, Sophie Fanelli, Maggie Farrar, Joan Green, Lyle Kirtman, Tony MacKay, Steve Munby, Carlye Olsen, Glen Price, Jonathan Raymond, Laura Schwalm, Lyn Sharratt, Claude St. Cyr, Sandy Thorstenson, Sue Walsh, Jay Westover, and Greg Whitby.

If you go by the rule that 80% of the best breakthrough ideas come from leading practitioners, as I do, you have to love leaders at all levels: policymakers, students and teachers, school, district and system leaders, community advocates and more. There are heaps of them for me, and I can only name the main countries: Australia, Canada (all provinces), China (Hong Kong), Finland, Netherlands, New Zealand, Uruguay, and the United States (especially California). And within these countries we have countless co-conspirators working, making the moral purpose of equity a reality. I wish I could name all those from these countries who contributed, but it would fill several pages. All of this work focuses on grounded system change in close partnership with all levels—a breeding ground for nuanced ideas.

There are also some academics who disguise themselves as leading practitioners whom I have the privilege of learning from: Bruce Alberts, Sir Michael Barber, Simon Breakspear, Carol Campbell, Linda Darling-Hammond, John Hattie, Andy Hargreaves, Ken Leithwood, Pak Tee Ng, Pedro Noguera, Sir Ken Robinson, Pasi Sahlberg, Andreas Schleicher, Dennis Shirley, and Michael Stevenson.

I am grateful for our major foundation sponsors and funders: the Stuart Foundation and the Hewlett Foundation. We could not have sustained our work without you.

Then there is the Corwin team: finely honed, ever better, worldwide movers, lovely to work with. They are family: Mike Soules, Lisa Shaw, Arnis Burvikovs, Desirée Bartlett, Melanie Birdsall, Eliza Erickson, Taryn Waters, and Lynne Curry. Corwin—a pulsating force for good.

Speaking of family, I have a real one, and they are gems each and every one, and as a group. They are more than I deserve, but I will take them and run. A monster thanks to Wendy, who can knock and nuance with the best of them. And to my two youngest sons who are just getting into formation: Bailey and Conor. I am so loving being an intimate part of your evolution and growth.

All in all, I should be so lucky!

about the author

Michael Fullan, OC, is the former Dean of the Ontario Institute for Studies in Education and Professor Emeritus of the University of Toronto. He is co-leader of the New Pedagogies for Deep Learning global initiative (npdl .global). Recognized as a worldwide authority on educational reform, he advises policymakers and local leaders in helping to achieve the moral purpose of all children learning. Michael Fullan received the Order of Canada in December 2012. He holds honorary doctorates from several universities around the world.

Fullan is a prolific, award-winning author whose books have been published in many languages. His book *Leading in a Culture of Change* received the 2002 Book of the Year Award by Learning Forward. *Breakthrough* (with Peter Hill and Carmel Crévola) won the 2006 Book of the Year Award from the American Association of Colleges for Teacher Education (AACTE), and *Turnaround Leadership in Higher Education* (with Geoff Scott) won the Bellwether Book Award in 2009. *Change Wars* (with Andy Hargreaves) was named the 2009 Book of the Year by Learning Forward, and *Professional Capital* (with Andy Hargreaves) won the AACTE 2013 Book of the Year and the Grawemeyer Award in Education in 2015.

Michael Fullan's latest books are *The Principal: Three Keys for Maximizing Impact*; *Coherence: The Right Drivers in Action for Schools, Districts, and Systems* (with Joanne Quinn); *Deep Learning: Engage the World*

Change the World (with Joanne Quinn and Joanne McEachen); *Surreal Change: The Real Life of Transforming Public Education* (autobiography); and *Nuance: Why Some Leaders Succeed and Others Fail*.

For more information on books, articles, and videos, please go to www.michaelfullan.ca.

A SAGE Publishing Company

Helping educators make the greatest impact

CORWIN HAS ONE MISSION: to enhance education through intentional professional learning.

We build long-term relationships with our authors, educators, clients, and associations who partner with us to develop and continuously improve the best evidence-based practices that establish and support lifelong learning.

The Ontario Principals' Council (OPC) is a voluntary professional association representing 5,000 practising school leaders in elementary and secondary schools across Ontario. We believe that exemplary leadership results in outstanding schools and improved student achievement. We foster quality leadership through world-class professional services and supports, striving to continuously achieve **"quality leadership—our principal product."**

bcpʘvpa

Serving members by supporting effective leadership in education through representation, advocacy and leadership development

The B.C. Principals' and Vice-Principals' Association (BCPVPA) is a voluntary professional association representing more than 2,500 school leaders employed as principals and vice-principals in British Columbia's public education system. The BCPVPA provides its members with the professional services and support they need to provide exemplary leadership in public education and foster success in student learning.

CORWIN LEADERSHIP

Anthony Kim & Alexis Gonzales-Black
Designed to foster flexibility and continuous innovation, this resource expands cutting-edge management and organizational techniques to empower schools with the agility and responsiveness vital to their new environment.

Jonathan Eckert
Explore the collective and reflective approach to progress, process, and programs that will build conditions that lead to strong leadership and teaching, which will improve student outcomes.

PJ Caposey
Offering a fresh perspective on teacher evaluation, this book guides administrators to transform their school culture and evaluation process to improve teacher practice and, ultimately, student achievement.

Dwight L. Carter & Mark White
Through understanding the past and envisioning the future, the authors use practical exercises and real-life examples to draw the blueprint for adapting schools to the age of hyper-change.

Raymond L. Smith & Julie R. Smith
This solid, sustainable, and laser-sharp focus on instructional leadership strategies for coaching might just be your most impactful investment toward student achievement.

Simon T. Bailey & Marceta F. Reilly
This engaging resource provides a simple, sustainable framework that will help you move your school from mediocrity to brilliance.

Debbie Silver & Dedra Stafford
Equip educators to develop resilient and mindful learners primed for academic growth and personal success.

Peter Gamwell & Jane Daly
Discover a new perspective on how to nurture creativity, innovation, leadership, and engagement.

Leadership That Makes an Impact

Steven Katz, Lisa Ain Dack, & John Malloy

Leverage the oppositional forces of top-down expectations and bottom-up experience to create an intelligent, responsive school.

Peter M. DeWitt

Centered on staff efficacy, these resources present discussion questions, vignettes, strategies, and action steps to improve school climate, leadership collaboration, and student growth.

Eric Sheninger

Harness digital resources to create a new school culture, increase communication and student engagement, facilitate real-time professional growth, and access new opportunities for your school.

Russell J. Quaglia, Kristine Fox, Deborah Young, Michael J. Corso, & Lisa L. Lande

Listen to your school's voice to see how you can increase engagement, involvement, and academic motivation.

Michael Fullan, Joanne Quinn, & Joanne McEachen

Learn the right drivers to mobilize complex, coherent, whole-system change and transform learning for all students.

CORWIN LEADERSHIP